FOREWORD by Philip Sansone

President and Executive Director

The Whole Planet Foundation® cookbook was inspired by the experiences of our team while working and visiting with many of the almost 1,000,000 participating families in our microfinance projects from 60 partner countries.

During our regular monitoring and evaluation visits to these projects, as well as other team trips to our project communities, we are often invited by one of the families to share a meal featuring local traditional favorites. The hospitality from some of the world's poorest is amazing and reminds me of my days as a Peace Corps Volunteer, living and working on the Patuka River in Honduras with the Miskito Indians in the early 1970s. When visiting the villages on the Patuka, one family was always selected to provide my meals, for which of course, I paid. Having extra to spend on the meal, these meals were always more robust than a typical meal, as a chicken, fish or parrot was provided along with the beans, rice and my favorite, Miskito pan bread. Villagers used to crowd the windows and doorway to watch me eat. As hard as I would try, no one would join me until I had my fill. It was always a delicate balance of needing to eat enough to show appreciation for the food provided, yet not too much so that enough food would remain for the rest of the family. Forty-three years later, many of us today still have similar experiences when visiting poor communities where generosity and graciousness are in abundance.

WHOLE PLANET FOUNDATION TEAM
Back row from left to right: JP Kloninger, Evan Lambert, Steve Wanta, Genie Bolduc, Daniel Vidal, Daniel Zoltani, Lauren Evans, Brian Doe, Claire Kelly, Armando Huerta, Victor Quiroz. Front row from left to right: Morgan Peretti, Philip Sansone, Joy Stoddard, Lee Valkenaar, Alyssa Manse. *Photo courtesy of Whole Foods Market's Ha Lam.*

Even though the entire team contributed, this book would not have been possible without the leadership, management and editing provided by Joy Stoddard, our Director of Development and Outreach. It was only through her labor of love that this book exists. The recipes we have collected for this book are just a few of our favorites. We hope you enjoy them and the stories of the women who gave them to us.

Philip Sansone
President and Executive Director
Whole Planet Foundation

TABLE OF CONTENTS

WHOLE PLANET
FOUNDATION

ABOUT THE RECIPES IN THIS BOOK

The recipes of *Liberation Soup* begin with fascinating stories and photos along with personal and cultural traditions from inspiring microentrepreneurs supported by Whole Planet Foundation®. Many of the recipes are then tested and developed by Whole Foods Market®'s culinary content editors, Kate Rowe and Molly Siegler, who get to peek into kitchens around the world to discover new ingredients, learn different techniques and catch a glimpse of cooking in a variety of places and cultures. Field notes and photos, taken by the Whole Planet Foundation team while visiting the microentrepreneurs, serve as the starting point of the culinary team's research into the dishes. Some clients provide fully written recipes that Kate and Molly test and adjust. They compare the recipes and concepts to traditional dishes from the home countries and stay true to tradition while editing the recipes in a style familiar to Whole Foods Market shoppers.

Other recipes in this book include just the name of a dish and list of ingredients written by the microentrepreneurs, or simply a basic description of the finished dish. Look for this seal that marks these recipes as *For the Adventurous and Curious: Sharing Culinary Culture.* Connect with us on social media and share your experience of recreating the recipe in your kitchen, using #WPFIntheKitchen. We are excited to hear how you prepared your meal, your suggestions, what you learned, what you liked and did not like according to your taste buds, and perhaps even a story about a meal that inspires you and the culinary traditions of your family. We also encourage you to visit *wholeplanetfoundation.org/recipes* for videos, photos and bonus recipes.

Finally, we would like to share with you our best advocate, the Whole Trade® program. One percent of sales of Whole Trade products sold in Whole Foods Market is donated to Whole Planet Foundation. Look for recipes from countries where Whole Trade products originate. Whole Planet Foundation is alleviating poverty there specifically because Whole Foods Market buys those products. The recipes for Spinach Cakes (*Pastelitos de Espinaca*) from Ecuador, and Haitian Pumpkin Soup (*Soup Joumou*), known as Liberation Soup, are two examples.

Most importantly, we want those who may not otherwise have access to these cultural food preparations to be able to make these dishes at home. Our goal is for the recipes to create a connection between you and the microentrepreneurs supported and championed by Whole Planet Foundation. Enjoy!

¡Buen provecho! Bon appétit! Svadist Khana! Afiyet Olsun! An Nyon Nhe! Tayo'y Magsikain! Koh Hai Cha-roen Ar-harn! Selamat makan! Ufurahie chakula chako!

From Ecuador to Chile, South Africa to Burkina Faso to Kenya and Ethiopia, Fiji to Samoa and Indonesia to Bangladesh, our Whole Planet Foundation team including Evan Lambert, Brian Doe, Genie Bolduc and Daniel Zoltani have met with microcredit clients to capture recipes like **KENYAN-STYLE KALE AND TOMATOES**. If Kenyan microentrepreneur Godfrey runs out of money at the end of the week, he feeds his family this *Sukuma Wiki* dish which in Swahili means *push the week*, because kale is nutrient dense. When Genie Bolduc and Joy Stoddard visited Godfrey's farm, they had the pleasure of meeting his wife, daughter, mother and a family friend. After a tour of the small family farm, they all gathered into the shade for an afternoon snack of water, soda, arrowroot and sweet bananas. Godfrey proudly pointed out the water well he created for irrigation, explaining how he dug 144 feet deep into the ground with basic tools and his bare hands. Godfrey is smart, capable, industrious and motivated to lift his family out of poverty. We hope you enjoy learning about the international side dishes described in this chapter, along with the personal successes of the inspiring entrepreneurs you support.

Top photo courtesy of Crystal Thompson.
Bottom photo courtesy of Whole Planet Foundation's Evan Lambert.
Opposite Page: Photo courtesy of Whole Planet Foundation's Brian Doe.

SIDES

Pastelitos de Espinaca

Photos courtesy of Whole Planet Foundation's Evan Lambert.

Lucia, Ecuador

BUSINESS: neighborhood restaurant

Lucia is a microcredit client in the Imbabura province of Ecuador where Whole Foods Market sources Whole Trade® roses. Through Whole Planet Foundation's partner FODEMI, Lucia sells her well-known *almuerzos* (lunches) for $1.75, including soup and *seco* (rice with meat, salad and a side). Her customers tell her this is expensive! She serves these lovely spinach pancakes as one of her side dishes. She opened her restaurant three years ago and was very nervous at first. Her brother worked construction, and he and the crew would pre-order lunches from her. This was guaranteed business and helped mitigate her risk as a new startup. Lucia used her first loan as seed capital for the restaurant and her most recent loan to purchase a new stove and invest in plates and kitchen wares. Her children help out in the kitchen when they are not at school or studying. She says they are all better off now because she has money to buy her children school clothes and food. Learn more about Lucia and other entrepreneurs at *wholeplanetfoundation.org.*

WHOLE PLANET
FOUNDATION®

SPINACH CAKES

Whole Foods Market® tested recipe

(SERVES 6)

These Ecuadorian-inspired green pancakes flavored with a hint of cilantro are a perfect complement to a savory meal. This recipe was inspired by Lucia, a microcredit client of Whole Planet Foundation's microfinance partner FODEMI in Ecuador.

1 tablespoon plus 2 teaspoons canola oil, divided

½ cup chopped sweet onion

1 (10-ounce) package frozen chopped spinach, thawed and drained well

3 tablespoons chopped fresh cilantro

1¼ cups all-purpose flour

1 teaspoon baking powder

½ teaspoon fine sea salt

3 eggs

1 cup milk

- In a large skillet, heat 1 tablespoon of the oil over medium-high heat.

- Add onion and cook 5 to 6 minutes or until tender and browned.

- Stir in spinach and cilantro and remove from heat. Let cool.

- In a large bowl, whisk together flour, baking powder and salt.

- In a small bowl, whisk together eggs and milk.

- Whisk egg mixture into flour mixture until blended.

- Stir in cooled spinach mixture just until evenly blended.

- In a large skillet, heat 1 teaspoon of the oil over medium-high heat until hot.

- Drop pancake batter by scant ¼ cupfuls and cook 1 to 2 minutes per side or until golden on both sides.

- Add more oil and adjust heat as needed.

- Repeat with remaining batter.

ECUADOR

Photo courtesy of Whole Planet Foundation's Evan Lambert.

Empanadas de Aceituna, Huevo y Carne

Mariana, Chile

BUSINESS: making and selling empanadas

Mariana is a microcredit client in the Temuco region of southern Chile where Whole Foods Market sources blueberries. This area has higher than average poverty rates, and prior to 2010 when the project began, there were many impoverished entrepreneurs like Mariana who had never taken a loan before because they do not qualify for traditional bank loans. Through Whole Planet Foundation's partner Fundación Banigualdad, Mariana received her first loan of $140, which she used to purchase ingredients and cooking materials. Since taking her first loan, she has built a reputation for making high quality *empanadas* and is kept busy by regular customers. Mariana says that even though these are small loans, they are a big help because before she didn't have access to any money at all. Now she dreams of having her own house. Learn more about Mariana and other entrepreneurs at *wholeplanetfoundation.org*.

Photos courtesy of Whole Planet Foundation's Steve Wanta.

OLIVE, EGG AND BEEF EMPANADAS

Whole Foods Market® tested recipe

SERVES 8

These Chilean empanadas are easy to make and sure to be a favorite. The dough is easy to handle and the filling is flavorful with beef, tomatoes, olives and hard-cooked eggs. Baking the empanadas gives them a crisp texture without frying. This recipe was inspired by Mariana, a microcredit client of Whole Planet Foundation's microfinance partner Fundación Banigualdad in Chile.

2½ cups all-purpose flour, plus more for rolling dough

1 teaspoon fine sea salt

½ cup (1 stick) cold unsalted butter, cut into small pieces

2 egg yolks, divided

1 tablespoon canola oil

1 medium onion, chopped

1 pound ground beef

1 (14.5-ounce) can diced tomatoes

½ cup pitted Kalamata olives, chopped

4 eggs, hard-cooked, peeled and cut into quarters

CHILE

- In a large bowl, whisk together flour and salt. Cut in butter with a pastry blender or 2 knives.

- In a small bowl, whisk together 1 egg yolk and ½ cup water. Stir into bowl with flour mixture until evenly blended.

- Turn dough out onto a floured surface and knead until smooth.

- Cover and refrigerate dough for 1 hour.

- In a large skillet, heat oil over medium-high heat until hot. Add onion and cook 6 to 8 minutes or until onion is browned and soft. Reduce heat to medium.

- Stir in beef, tomatoes and olives and cook 10 to 12 minutes or until beef is browned and liquid has evaporated.

- Preheat the oven to 425°F. Line a baking sheet with parchment paper.

- Cut dough into 16 equal pieces. On a lightly floured surface, roll out each piece of dough to a circle 5-inches in diameter.

- Place about 2 tablespoons beef filling in the center of each circle and top with a piece of hard-cooked egg.

- Brush the outside edge of dough with water and fold in half over filling. Press firmly to seal.

- Place empanadas on the prepared baking sheet. In a small bowl, whisk together remaining egg yolk and 1 tablespoon water. Brush empanadas with egg wash and bake 30 minutes or until golden brown.

Atchar

Top photo courtesy of Whole Foods Market's Ha Lam.
Bottom photo courtesy of Whole Planet Foundation's Brian Doe.

Joyce, South Africa

BUSINESS: food vendor

Joyce is a microcredit client in Mpumalanga, South Africa where Whole Foods Market sources dried mangoes and Whole Trade® citrus. In South Africa's Limpopo and Mpumalanga provinces, fruit grows in abundance and the dried mangoes sold in Whole Foods Market stores originate here. *Atchar* derives from the Indian influence on South African cuisine. In Hindi atchar means pickle. Atchar is a relish or salad-like side served with other dishes made out of mangoes, chillies and olive oil. It was brought to South Africa by Indian immigrants but is now eaten by the main population, especially in the areas where Whole Planet Foundation is supporting impoverished women. Learn more about Joyce and other entrepreneurs at *wholeplanetfoundation.org*.

SOUTH AFRICAN-INSPIRED PICKLED MANGO

Whole Foods Market® tested recipe

MAKES ABOUT
3.5 CUPS

This sweet-and-sour mango condiment is based on South African **ATCHAR**, pickled mango. Traditionally it's left out in the sun for a couple weeks to age but ours can be enjoyed the next day. The pickle's assertive flavor will intensify as the mango softens. Serve with grilled meats and curried vegetables or simply with brown rice. This recipe was inspired by Joyce, a microcredit client of Whole Planet Foundation's microfinance partner Small Enterprise Foundation in South Africa.

½ cup balsamic vinegar

¼ cup honey

2 cloves garlic, finely chopped

2 teaspoons chili powder

2 teaspoons curry powder

1 teaspoon ground cumin

1 teaspoon ground ginger

1 teaspoon mustard seeds

½ teaspoon fine sea salt

2 tablespoons extra-virgin olive oil

2 unripe (firm) mangoes, peeled and flesh cut into ½-inch chunks

- Place vinegar, honey, garlic, chili powder, curry powder, cumin, ginger, mustard seeds and salt in a medium saucepan and heat to a boil over medium-high heat.

- Reduce heat to medium and simmer 5 to 6 minutes or until thickened and reduced, stirring occasionally. Watch carefully so mixture doesn't burn.

- Remove from heat and whisk in oil.

- Stir in mango and set aside to let cool.

- Refrigerate at least 8 hours or overnight before serving.

- The pickle can be refrigerated for up to a week.

SOUTH
AFRICA

Photo of Whole Planet Foundation's Brian Doe in South Africa courtesy of Small Enterprise Foundation.

Sukuma Wiki

Godfrey, Kenya
BUSINESS: small farm

Godfrey is a microcredit client in Kenya where Whole Foods Market sources coffee through Allegro Coffee Company®. Through Jamii Bora Trust, Whole Planet Foundation's first partner in Kenya, Godfrey's first loan was the equivalent of $129, which he used to buy manure and his first cow. His second loan was $258 and he used it to buy another cow. Godfrey has had his farm for 24 years and grew up seeing his parents grow crops, so he has a good yield of coffee and leafy greens including kale. If he runs out of money at the end of the week, he feeds his family *Sukuma Wiki* which in Swahili means *push the week*, because kale is so nutrient-dense. Godfrey is a hard worker who provides for his wife, young daughter and mother. Godfrey explained that microcredit has enabled him to diversify his farm for continued income and food for his family. Learn more about Godfrey and other entrepreneurs at *wholeplanetfoundation.org*.

Top photo courtesy of Whole Foods Market's Ha Lam.
Bottom photo courtesy of Whole Planet Foundation's Genie Bolduc.

KENYAN-STYLE KALE AND TOMATOES

Whole Foods Market® tested recipe

(SERVES 4)

In Kenya, this popular dish, called **SUKUMA WIKI** is eaten without utensils and relies on **CHAPATI** (a variety of flatbread) or **UGALI** (Swahili for a steamed corn staple) to scoop up bites instead. This recipe was inspired by Godfrey, a microcredit client of Whole Planet Foundation's first microfinance partner in Kenya, Jamii Bora Trust.

2 teaspoons canola oil

1 yellow onion, chopped

1 jalapeño pepper, seeded and finely chopped (optional)

3 ripe but firm tomatoes, chopped

2 bunches kale or collard greens (about 1 pound total), ribs removed, leaves thinly sliced

2 tablespoons lemon juice

¼ teaspoon fine sea salt

¼ teaspoon ground black pepper

- Heat oil in a large pot over medium heat.

- Add onion and jalapeño (if using) and cook, stirring often, until softened and golden brown, 7 to 8 minutes.

- Add tomatoes and cook until collapsed and juicy, about 10 minutes more.

- Add kale, ½ cup water, lemon juice, salt and pepper, toss once or twice, cover and simmer, stirring occasionally, until kale is tender, 10 to 15 minutes.

- Spoon into bowls and serve.

KENYA

Photo courtesy of Whole Planet Foundation's Genie Bolduc.

Baigani Tavuteke

Rosie, Fiji

BUSINESS: making and selling jewelry

Rosie is a microcredit client in Fiji where Whole Foods Market sources fish. Through Whole Planet Foundation's partner South Pacific Business Development (Fiji), Rosie is currently on her second loan and serves as Center Chief, a leadership role in her borrower group. She utilizes the loans to support her small business making jewelry which she started in 2006. Due to the loan services provided by South Pacific Business Development over the past few years, Rosie has been able to grow her business by purchasing additional materials to increase her inventory. Recent Hollywood movies featuring Fiji have brought more tourism to the island. Rosie says, *"I am able to sell my merchandise to tourists for a higher price and can finally expand my business."* Learn more about Rosie and other entrepreneurs at *wholeplanetfoundation.org*.

Photos courtesy of Whole Planet Foundation's Daniel Zoltani.

WHOLE PLANET
FOUNDATION

EGGPLANT FRITTERS

Whole Foods Market® tested recipe

SERVES 4-6

These simple eggplant fritters served with coconut-caramelized onions are a traditional snack or side dish in Fiji. The onions can either be cooked in the remaining oil from making the fritters or in a separate skillet to save time. This recipe was inspired by Rosie, a microcredit client of Whole Planet Foundation's microfinance partner South Pacific Business Development Microfinance (Fiji) Ltd.

1 large eggplant (about 1 pound)
1 cup all-purpose flour
1 teaspoon fine sea salt
¾ cup canola oil
1 large onion, thinly sliced
½ cup coconut cream, skimmed from the
  top of a chilled can of coconut milk

- Cut eggplant in half lengthwise.
- Cut each half crosswise in ¼-inch-thick slices.
- Spread slices in a single layer on a baking sheet lined with paper towels and pat dry.
- In a medium bowl, whisk together flour, salt and 1 cup water to make a thick batter.
- Preheat the oven to 250°F.
- In a large skillet or wok, heat oil over medium-high heat until hot.
- Dip eggplant slices in batter and cook in oil, 3 to 4 minutes per side, until golden brown.
- Transfer to a baking sheet and keep warm in the oven.
- Repeat with remaining eggplant slices and batter.
- Pour all but 1 tablespoon of oil from the skillet.
- Add onion to the skillet and cook about 8 minutes or until golden brown, stirring occasionally.
- Stir in coconut cream and remove from heat.
- Serve onion mixture with eggplant fritters.

FIJI

Photo courtesy of Whole Planet Foundation's Daniel Zoltani.

Fa'alifu Fa'i

Photos courtesy of Whole Planet Foundation's Daniel Zoltani.

Charity, Samoa

BUSINESS: restaurant owner and operator

Charity is a microcredit client from the Samoan island of Upolu, where Whole Foods Market sources bigeye and yellowfin tuna. Through Whole Planet Foundation's partner South Pacific Business Development (Samoa), Charity utilized her first loan to open her new restaurant named Sameyna's (a combination of her three daughters' first names), purchasing tables, a rice cooker and a blender. Charity has loved cooking since she was a young girl but only recently was able to do it to generate income. Her restaurant is located in the front room of her home which she begins to prepare at 7 o'clock and opens for business at 11 o'clock in the morning every Monday through Saturday. She offers a seasonal menu based on the fruits and vegetables available at the local market. Currently she makes a soup daily and serves a meal of chicken curry with sausage and banana or rice. Charity is very proud of her restaurant and reputation as a business owner. She is also grateful to be able to share this experience with her family who often helps in the kitchen. Learn more about Charity and other entrepreneurs at *wholeplanetfoundation.org*.

SAMOAN GREEN BANANAS IN COCONUT SAUCE

Whole Foods Market® tested recipe

SERVES 6–8

This recipe is based on **Fa'alifu Fa'i**, a ubiquitous side dish in Samoa where the unripe bananas are called "green beans." It's deliciously mild, but you can also serve the bananas with lime wedges, cilantro or chili-garlic paste. This recipe was inspired by Charity's fellow entrepreneur Lusia and served by Charity, a microcredit client of Whole Planet Foundation's microfinance partner South Pacific Business Development Microfinance (Samoa) Ltd.

6 green (unripe) bananas, peeled
1 (13.5-ounce) can coconut milk
½ medium onion, diced
¼ teaspoon fine sea salt

- Fill a large pot ⅔ full with water and bring to a boil.
- Add bananas and boil until they are just soft when pierced with a knife, about 5 minutes.
- Drain bananas well. Set aside.
- Add coconut milk, onion and salt to the same pot and bring to a boil.
- Lower heat to a simmer and add bananas.
- Cook, uncovered, until coconut milk thickens and bananas begin to break into large pieces, about 10 minutes.
- Serve warm.

 SAMOA

Photos courtesy of Whole Planet Foundation's Daniel Zoltani.

Indonesian Crispies

Ona, Indonesia

BUSINESS: food vendor

Ona is a microcredit client in Banda Aceh, Indonesia where Whole Foods Market sources **Whole Trade**® coffee through Allegro Coffee Company®. Through Whole Planet Foundation's partner KOMIDA, Ona was able to expand her business selling *Crispy* (Fried Cow Skin), a family business that was passed down from her parents. Her mother and father began producing and selling *Crispy* in 1989, generating a profit which supported their family. With her second loan of $218, Ona was able to purchase certain additions to the equipment she already owned to help facilitate the process of drying the meat. In the future Ona would like to expand the business to other areas outside of Banda Aceh. Learn more about Ona and other entrepreneurs at *wholeplanetfoundation.org*.

Photos courtesy of Whole Planet Foundation's Daniel Zoltani.

FRIED COW SKIN

INDONESIAN CRISPIES is Ona's business of making and selling fried cow skin, after she has dried it under the sun on her rooftop. Her dehydration system, shown below, is a flat bed made of wood, wire and mesh. Ona is a microcredit client of Whole Planet Foundation's microfinance partner KOMIDA in Indonesia. As KOMIDA demonstrates its ability and capacity as a leading microfinance institution in Indonesia, Whole Planet Foundation is continuing to support KOMIDA, funding five new branches in Borneo and West Java. The support will disburse $6.5 million in collateral-free microcredit loans for 10,000 new clients like Ona who will have a chance at a better life through entrepreneurship.

Dried cow skin
Vegetable oil

- First, Ona dries the skin under the sun.
- Then, the skin is fried in oil and drained.
- The chips are served like onion rings.

INDONESIA

Photo courtesy of Whole Planet Foundation's Daniel Zoltani.

Zapallo Italiano

Photos courtesy of Whole Planet Foundation's Evan Lambert.

Deborah, Chile

BUSINESS: small restaurant

Deborah is a microcredit client in the Temuco region of southern Chile where Whole Foods Market sources juices. Her town is on the way down to Puerto Montt which is the famous jumping off point for visiting Patagonia. Through Whole Planet Foundation's partner Fundación Banigualdad, Deborah runs a restaurant called *de Dulce y Salado,* which means of sweet and salty, and she makes traditional dishes such as *Aji de Pollo,* or spicy chicken and *Zapallo Italiano,* which she serves with a salad and fries. Her business is seasonal, as the period of summer vacations in January and February is a slow time for her while most people are out of town. Silver production is prevalent in the Temuco region, as can be seen by her beautiful necklace and ornaments. She decided to open her own restaurant as an alternative to being a housekeeper and working in silver. Deborah's loan enabled her to invest in chairs and tables for her restaurant, and with a future loan, she plans to buy an oven. Learn more about Deborah and other entrepreneurs at *wholeplanetfoundation.org.*

STUFFED ZUCCHINI

This simple dish is beloved in Deborah's neighborhood because the Chileans in her area adore everything with the colors of the Italian flag: red, green and white. This **ZAPALLO ITALIANO** is Deborah's recipe and one of her most healthy vegetable and beef dishes, prepared her way, without "too much sweet and salty". Deborah is a microcredit client of Whole Planet Foundation's microfinance partner Fundación Banigualdad in Chile. Serve with salad and fries, the way Deborah prefers it.

Zucchini
Ground beef
Rice
Salt
Pepper
Ketchup
Mint

- Hollow out the zucchini.
- Combine the ground beef, rice, salt, pepper, ketchup and mint.
- Cook for 30 minutes.
- Cool the mixture.
- Stuff zucchinis and serve.

CHILE

Buna Qala

Atsede, Ethiopia

BUSINESS: making and selling coffee chew

Atsede is a microcredit client in Ethiopia where Whole Foods Market sources **Whole Trade®** coffee through Allegro Coffee Company®. Through Whole Planet Foundation's partner OCSSCO, Atsede takes loans averaging $150 for "fattening" which means buying a young cow and raising it to sell at a profit. The more expensive the cow, the older the animal is and the less time it will take to raise. With each subsequent loan Atsede still only buys one cow, but it is just a bit older than the first one and thus can be sold quicker to turn the profit faster. Atsede says that her only goal is to keep a steady and dependable profit from the business. When asked to explain why she raises cows, she says that she is too old to travel back and forth to the market to trade goods, but raising the cows can be done at home and gives her enough steady profit to support herself and not have to rely on her children. Learn more about Atsede and other entrepreneurs at *wholeplanetfoundation.org*.

Photos courtesy of Whole Planet Foundation's Steve Wanta.

WHOLE PLANET
FOUNDATION®

ETHIOPIAN COFFEE CHEW

This **BUNA QALA** is Atsede's recipe from Ethiopia, where coffee is a foodstuff as well as an important beverage to the culture. The tradition is to leave the **BUNA QALA** (coffee chew) on the side of your mouth for hours to provide fuel for the hard work ahead. Atsede is a microcredit client of Whole Planet Foundation's microfinance partner OCSSCO in Ethiopia.

Green coffee beans
Barley
Butter
Sugar

- Roast "green" coffee on a wok over an open flame.
- Add barley, continue to roast.
- Add butter.
- Add sugar.
- Heap into a bowl and serve by the handful.

ETHIOPIA

Photo courtesy of Whole Planet Foundation's Brian Doe.

Soumbala

Photos courtesy of Whole Planet Foundation's Brian Doe.

Djeinaba, Burkina Faso

BUSINESS: roadside restaurant

Djeinaba (left) is a microcredit client in the southwest province of Burkina Faso where Whole Foods Market sources shea nuts for shea butter. Djeinaba's small roadside restaurant serves primarily lunch, and largely dishes that use the popular *soumbala* (pictured in the upper right photo), which is fermented locust bean. Soumbala is an inexpensive source of protein served with meat, dried fish or rice cooked with tomatoes, garlic and spices. Through Whole Planet Foundation's partner GRAINE, Djeinaba's four microcredit loans have enabled her to stock her restaurant, and the current loan of $140 pays for two helpers. Soumbala can be difficult to procure in the United States, but tamarind is an alternative for this spice. Learn more about Djeinaba and other entrepreneurs at *wholeplanetfoundation.org*.

BURKINA FASO SOUMBALA CONDIMENT

This is Djeinaba's **SOUMBALA** recipe of the popular fermented locust bean she serves in her restaurant. The beans are formed into a paste and dried to use in recipes. Despite its strong smell, soumbala is an excellent condiment that enhances the taste of many West African sauces. Djeinaba is a microcredit client of Whole Planet Foundation's microfinance partner GRAINE in Burkina Faso. Serve with smoked fish in a tomato, onion, chili and bay leaf sauce, the way Djeinaba prefers it.

Rice
Soumbala
Garlic
Onion
Salt and pepper
Bouillon cubes
Vegetable oil
Smoked Fish

- Steam the rice and set aside.
- Crush together the soumbala, garlic, onion, pepper, salt and 1 bouillon cube.
- Set aside the paste.
- Heat the oil in a pot and add the amount of water necessary to cook the rice.
- Add salt, another bouillon cube and smoked fish.
- Once the sauce begins to boil, add the rice and cook.
- Put the soumbala paste in the middle of rice.
- Cook over low heat for 15 minutes.
- Serve hot.

BURKINA FASO

Tihove, Pap, Maxoja Worms, Matsawa, Guxe, & Tinyawa

Photos courtesy of Whole Planet Foundation's Brian Doe.

Anna, South Africa

BUSINESS: roadside restaurant

Anna is a microcredit client in Mupumalanga, South Africa where Whole Foods Market sources Whole Trade® citrus. Through Whole Planet Foundation's microfinance partner Small Enterprise Foundation, Anna took her first loan of $150 to purchase new pots and kitchen equipment to serve more people at her restaurant situated on the road leading to the gates of the Krueger National Park. Anna was positive about utilizing credit, along with a healthy amount of skepticism, and said that when she first got the loan she was very nervous about being taken advantage of. She is a single lady living with her two children and three grandchildren in her house that is located just behind the restaurant. For her second loan, Anna borrowed $150 to buy foodstuffs in bulk at a lower cost, deciding not to borrow more money than the first year, a sign that she is still very careful about assessing her need for credit. Her business is growing, and she has been able to add eggs and chicken, high profit items that need up front capital to purchase a meaningful quantity. Learn more about Anna and other entrepreneurs at *wholeplanetfoundation.org*.

TRADITIONAL SOUTH AFRICAN SIDE DISHES

TIHOVE, PAP, MAXOJA WORMS, MATSAWA, GUXE and TINYAWA are dishes Anna prepares in her restaurant. From the photo to the left, follow this South African meal clockwise from the white bean dish in the top center. These dishes are typical of the Mupumalanga area in that they all utilize ground peanuts in place of oil. Anna is a microcredit client of Whole Planet Foundation's microfinance partner Small Enterprise Foundation in South Africa.

- *Tihove* is the top center dish, a mixture of boiled white beans, maize (or corn) kernels and ground peanuts whose powder gives it a sauce-like consistency.

- *Pap* is to the right of Tihove and looks like four fluffy biscuits. Pap is a local wheat-like grain that is ground up and steamed into a solid starch which accompanies all meals in Mupumalanga.

- *Maxoja Worms* are dried worms that are boiled in water and mixed with the ground peanut powder.

- *Matsawa* is a side dish that is a mixture of boiled leaves and flowers from a pumpkin-like squash plant with the ground peanut powder.

- *Guxe,* or "South African okra," is another side dish of leaves that when boiled creates an okra-like sticky vegetarian dish.

- *Tinyawa* are shredded bean leaves with the ground peanut powder.

SOUTH AFRICA

Travel with us from Haiti to Guatemala to Bolivia, Colombia, Ecuador and Peru, Turkey onward to Kenya, and Thailand to Cambodia, for a culinary tour of comfort food and staple soups and stews with our team including Steve Wanta, Genie Bolduc, Evan Lambert, Brian Doe and Daniel Zoltani. When Steve and Genie visited microcredit client Norzina of our microfinance partner Fonkoze in Haiti, she shared her special recipe for **LIBERATION SOUP**, *Soup Joumou* in Kreyòl, the inspiration for the title of this cookbook. Genie and Steve went to the market with Norzina to purchase the soup ingredients and walked with Norzina to her home, where she prepared the soup and gave them a history lesson. Liberation Soup, she explained, is a special soup that celebrates Haitian independence. Whole Planet Foundation alleviates poverty through microcredit because it unleashes the entrepreneurial spirit in the very poor and empowers people to create or expand home-based businesses so that they can change their own lives through their own hard work and ingenuity. Cheers to you, Norzina!

Top and bottom right photos courtesy of Whole Planet Foundation's Genie Bolduc.
Bottom left and opposite page photos courtesy of Whole Planet Foundation's Daniel Zoltani.

SOUPS & STEWS

Soup Joumou

Norzina, Haiti

BUSINESS: selling charcoal and wood

Norzina is a microcredit client in Gonaives, Haiti where Whole Foods Market sources Whole Trade® mangoes. Through Whole Planet Foundation's partner Fonkoze, Norzina has a business on a back street behind the market where she sells charcoal in bulk to businesses, schools and individuals who then sell much smaller amounts at a time to others. Norzina supports her community by feeding the neighborhood children, setting an example of how to be successful and lift oneself out of poverty while helping others. When she can, Norzina feeds them Haitian Pumpkin Soup, or *Soup Joumou* know as Liberation Soup, the inspiration for this cookbook. **Thank you Norzina.** Learn more about Norzina and other entrepreneurs at *wholeplanetfoundation.org*.

Top photo courtesy of Whole Foods Market's Ha Lam.
Bottom photo courtesy of Whole Planet Foundation's Genie Bolduc.

WHOLE PLANET
FOUNDATION®

HAITIAN PUMPKIN SOUP

Whole Foods Market® tested recipe

SERVES 8

Haitian households celebrate their country's Independence Day with bowls of this comforting soup. The national holiday falls on New Year's Day, when Haitians walk from house to house to pay friends and family the first visits of the new year. Although this is a vegetarian version, add small cubes of browned beef stew meat along with the pumpkin, if you like. Simply remove and then return them to the pot just as you do the hot peppers. This recipe was inspired by Norzina, a microcredit client of Whole Planet Foundation's microfinance partner Fonkoze in Haiti.

7 cups cubed butternut squash or pumpkin
(about 2 pounds)

½ teaspoon fine sea salt

½ teaspoon ground black pepper

2 jalapeño or serrano peppers

10 whole cloves

4 carrots, peeled and sliced

2 turnips, peeled and cut into small chunks

½ small head green cabbage, cored and roughly chopped

½ teaspoon ground nutmeg

3 tablespoons lemon juice

¼ pound vermicelli or capellini

¼ cup chopped fresh parsley

- Put squash, 10 cups water, salt and pepper into a large pot.

- Stud peppers with cloves by pushing them halfway into the flesh, then add peppers to the pot, cover and bring to a boil.

- Reduce heat to medium low, cover and simmer until squash is very tender, 15 to 20 minutes.

- Transfer peppers to a small bowl and set aside.

- Working in batches, purée remaining contents of the pot in a blender or food processor until smooth, taking care as it will be very hot.

- Return puréed squash mixture to the pot along with peppers.

- Add carrots, turnips, cabbage, nutmeg and lemon juice, cover and bring to a boil.

- Reduce heat to medium low and simmer for 10 minutes.

- Stir in vermicelli and parsley, cover again and simmer gently until pasta is tender and soup is thickened, about 10 minutes more. Because the texture of squash and pumpkins can vary, thin the finished soup with a bit more water, if desired.

HAITI

Pepián

Anita, Guatemala

BUSINESS: small restaurant

Anita is a microcredit client in Guatemala where Whole Foods Market sources Whole Trade® coffee through Allegro Coffee Company®. Through Whole Planet Foundation's partner Banrural Grameen Guatemala, Anita started with a loan of $190 to invest in her small restaurant located in Sololá, just up the hill from the picturesque town of Panajachel overlooking Lake Atitlan. Anita is 56 years old and has been in the restaurant business for 17 years in various places. Anita's small but popular restaurant on the main street is where she sells lunch dishes like *Pepián*, as well as fried chicken, grilled meats and soups. Learn more about Anita and other entrepreneurs at *wholeplanetfoundation.org*.

Top photo courtesy of Whole Foods Market's Ha Lam.
Bottom photo courtesy of Whole Planet Foundation's Steve Wanta.

SPICED GUATEMALAN CHICKEN STEW WITH RICE

Whole Foods Market® tested recipe

SERVES 6

This flavorful stew combines pumpkin seeds, corn tortillas, chile peppers and tomatillos to make a rich sauce for chicken, but it could also be made with pork or beef. This recipe was inspired by Anita, a microcredit client of Whole Planet Foundation's microfinance partner Banrural Grameen Guatemala.

1 (3-pound) whole chicken, cut into 8 pieces, skin removed

3 cups chicken broth, divided

1 teaspoon fine sea salt

¼ cup pepitas (shelled pumpkin seeds)

¼ cup sesame seeds

1 teaspoon ground cinnamon

¼ teaspoon crushed red chile flakes

1 dried guajillo chile

1 (14.5-ounce) can diced tomatoes

5 medium tomatillos, husked and chopped

8 corn tortillas, divided

2 cups cooked long-grain white rice, for serving

- Place chicken, 2½ cups of the broth and salt in a large pot; bring to a boil.

- Reduce heat to medium-low and simmer 25 minutes, turning chicken over halfway through cooking.

- Meanwhile, heat a large skillet over medium heat until hot.

- Add pepitas, sesame seeds, cinnamon and chile flakes to the skillet and toast, stirring frequently, about 5 minutes or until fragrant.

- Remove from heat and place in a blender. Pulse until mixture resembles a powder.

- In the same skillet, toast guajillo chile until fragrant, about 30 seconds.

- Add remaining broth, tomatoes and tomatillos and bring to a boil.

- Reduce heat to medium and simmer until tender, about 10 minutes.

- Remove from heat and add to the blender with spice mixture.

- Tear 2 tortillas into large pieces, add to the blender with spices and tomato mixture and purée, taking care as the mixture will be hot.

- Pour purée into the pot with chicken, stir and continue to simmer 10 minutes or until chicken is cooked through and sauce is hot.

- Warm remaining tortillas and serve with chicken, sauce and rice.

GUATEMALA

Sopa de Quinoa y Verduras

Photos courtesy of Whole Planet Foundation's Evan Lambert.

Maria, Bolivia

BUSINESS: neighborhood restaurant

Maria is a microcredit client in the Potosí region of Bolivia where Whole Foods Market sources cacao and coffee through Allegro Coffee Company®. Potosí is the highest city in the world at well over 13,000 feet with frigid temperatures and a very harsh environment. Maria is one of the original microcredit clients with Whole Planet Foundation's partner Pro Mujer in Bolivia, repaying her 18th loan nine years after her first one. As the president of her borrower group, Maria is responsible for motivating the other clients and helping solve problems. She says that at times other women have had difficulties paying on time and she has had to help them pay. Maria understands this is part of the solidarity group lending methodology of microcredit, and while she might not like it, she understands the necessity. Maria says she has taken loans before with various other microfinance institutions and prefers to work with Pro Mujer because they *convive con ella,* or walk with her, whereas the other organizations are "pay and forget". Her advice is to save all you can and invest wisely. Learn more about Maria and other entrepreneurs at *wholeplanetfoundation.org.*

QUINOA VEGETABLE SOUP

Whole Foods Market® tested recipe

SERVES 6-8

A combination of vegetables and beef broth makes this Bolivian-inspired quinoa soup a tasty and satisfying meal. This recipe was inspired by Maria, a microcredit client of Whole Planet Foundation's microfinance partner Pro Mujer in Bolivia.

1 tablespoon canola oil

1 medium onion, finely chopped

2 cloves garlic, minced

3 plum tomatoes, chopped

1 red bell pepper, chopped

1 large turnip, peeled and cut into ½-inch pieces

½ cup quinoa, rinsed and drained

4 cups low-sodium beef broth

½ teaspoon fine sea salt

2 tablespoons chopped fresh parsley

- In a large saucepot, heat oil over medium-high heat until hot.

- Add onion and garlic and cook, stirring frequently, 6 to 8 minutes or until golden and soft.

- Stir in tomatoes, bell pepper, turnip, quinoa, broth, 1 cup water and salt.

- Bring to a boil over high heat.

- Reduce heat to medium-low, cover and cook 20 minutes or until quinoa is cooked and vegetables are tender.

- Stir in parsley.

BOLIVIA

Photo of Whole Planet Foundation's Evan Lambert in Bolivia courtesy of Pro Mujer.

Sopa de Cuchuco

Photos courtesy of Whole Planet Foundation's Evan Lambert.

Janet, Colombia

BUSINESS: restaurant

Janet is a microcredit client in Colombia where Whole Foods Market sources Whole Trade® flowers. Janet owns and operates a popular neighborhood restaurant called *La Mona*, which is known for serving a variety of daily menus based on typical Colombian food. A relatively new borrower of Whole Planet Foundation's partner Corporación Microcrédito Aval, Janet took her first loan in February 2011. She started with a $200 loan and now has a loan of $300. Her loan has provided working capital to cover business expenses such as menu ingredients and an outdoor barbecue. A few years ago, Janet endured a hard time during which she was robbed and her business was burned to the ground. She lost everything. At that time she took a loan from a loan shark to get back on her feet, but the interest was nearly 100%. Since then, through steady efforts, diligent work and the help of Corporación Microcrédito Aval, she has rebuilt her business and life. Learn more about Janet and other entrepreneurs at *wholeplanetfoundation.org*.

WHOLE PLANET
FOUNDATION®

BEEF AND BARLEY SOUP

Whole Foods Market® tested recipe

SERVES 6-8

This version of the traditional Colombian soup is primarily vegetables but gains substantial flavor from its base of beef broth and is thickened by barley flour. This recipe was inspired by Janet, a microcredit client of Whole Planet Foundation's microfinance partner Corporación Microcrédito Aval in Colombia.

1 tablespoon canola oil

1 medium onion, chopped

2 cloves garlic, minced

½ cup barley flour

4 cups low-sodium beef broth

1 (15-ounce) can lima or fava beans, rinsed and drained (about 1½ cups cooked beans)

2 large red potatoes, chopped (1 pound total)

2 carrots, chopped

2 cups shredded cabbage

¼ teaspoon fine sea salt

2 tablespoons chopped fresh cilantro

- In a large saucepot, heat oil over medium-high until hot.

- Add onion and garlic and cook 6 to 8 minutes or until browned.

- Stir in flour and cook 1 minute, stirring.

- Slowly add broth, 2 cups water and bring to a boil.

- Reduce heat to medium and simmer 15 minutes.

- Stir in beans, potatoes, carrots, cabbage and salt and bring to a boil.

- Reduce heat to medium and simmer 30 minutes longer or until vegetables are tender.

- Remove from heat and stir in cilantro.

COLOMBIA

Photo courtesy of Whole Planet Foundation's Evan Lambert.

Caldo de Bagre

Nelly, Ecuador

BUSINESS: restaurant

Nelly is a microcredit client in the Imbabura province of Ecuador where Whole Foods Market sources Whole Trade® roses. Nelly has been a microcredit client of Whole Planet Foundation's partner FODEMI since 2008, which has enabled her to run her own restaurant *Cevicheria El Rumbero*. With her loans, Nelly has managed to purchase a small pickup truck so that her son can drive her to Quito on Tuesdays and Fridays to pick up the fresh fish needed for her business. She says she likes to do that herself because she saves on transportation and delivery costs, and of course she picks only the best quality fish. Some of the dishes she prepares include crab, *encebollado*, *ceviche* and *Caldo de Bagre*, or fish soup. She sells the dishes for either 70 cents or $1.50 depending on the portion size her guest orders. Learn more about Nelly and other entrepreneurs at *wholeplanetfoundation.org*.

Photos courtesy of Whole Planet Foundation's Evan Lambert.

WHOLE PLANET
FOUNDATION®

FISH AND PEANUT SOUP

Whole Foods Market® tested recipe

SERVES 6-8

This rich and unusual fish soup from Ecuador is thickened by a combination of green plantains and peanuts. This recipe was inspired by Nelly, a microcredit client of Whole Planet Foundation's microfinance partner FODEMI in Ecuador.

¾ cup roasted unsalted peanuts

2 green plantains, chopped and divided

1 tablespoon canola oil

1 onion, chopped

2 cloves garlic, minced

1 teaspoon ground cumin

½ teaspoon fine sea salt

1 cup chopped cassava or yuca

1 pound catfish or tilapia fillets, cut into bite-sized pieces

3 tablespoons lime juice

3 tablespoons chopped fresh cilantro

- In a blender, purée peanuts, 1 plantain and 2 cups water.

- In a large saucepot, heat oil over medium-high until hot.

- Add onion and garlic and cook 6 minutes, stirring occasionally.

- Add cumin and cook 1 minute, stirring.

- Stir in peanut mixture, cassava, remaining plantain and 2 cups water and bring to a boil.

- Reduce heat to medium and simmer 10 minutes.

- Add fish and simmer 10 minutes longer or until fish is cooked through.

- Remove from heat and stir in lime juice and cilantro.

ECUADOR

Photo courtesy of Whole Planet Foundation's Evan Lambert.

Seco de Pollo en Salsa de Tomatillo

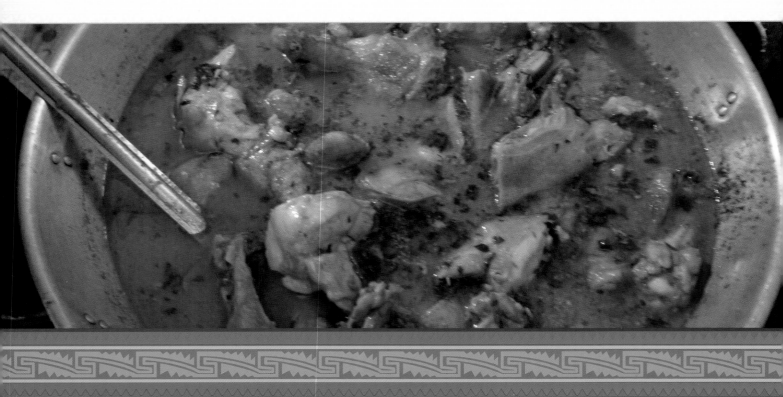

Photos courtesy of Whole Planet Foundation's Evan Lambert.

Lucia, Ecuador

BUSINESS: neighborhood restaurant

Lucia is a microcredit client in the Imbabura province of Ecuador where Whole Foods Market sources Whole Trade® roses. Lucia is 40 years old, married with four children and likes working for herself. Through Whole Planet Foundation's partner FODEMI, Lucia is able to operate her neighborhood restaurant, selling dishes like *Pastelitos de Espinaca* on page 6 and *Seco de Pollo en Salsa de Tomatillo*. Her lunches are popular and feature typical Ecuadorian cuisine. Lucia's restaurant offers a choice of soup made with chicken broth or chicken foot, or *menestra*, a potato-based soup, and a *seco*, or "dry" plate which is always a big pile of white rice, a small portion of meat, salad and a side of vegetables including perhaps more potatoes. Lucia often serves *seco de pollo*, chicken in a juice with simple onions and other vegetables, served over rice. Learn more about Lucia and other entrepreneurs at *wholeplanetfoundation.org*.

CHICKEN STEW WITH TOMATILLO SAUCE

Whole Foods Market® tested recipe

(SERVES 8)

Serve this stew over rice with corn tortillas on the side for soaking up the rich and tangy tomatillo and green onion sauce. If you like, use parsley as a flavorful substitute for the cilantro. For a more rustic version, serve the chicken on the bone. This recipe was inspired by Lucia, a microcredit client of Whole Planet Foundation's microfinance partner FODEMI in Ecuador.

1 pound tomatillos, husked and rinsed

4 bone-in, skinless chicken thighs (about 1½ pounds)

2 bone-in, skinless chicken breasts (about 1½ pounds)

1 to 2 jalapeño peppers, stemmed and halved lengthwise

½ teaspoon fine sea salt

1 tablespoon extra-virgin olive oil

½ cup roughly chopped fresh cilantro, plus more for garnish

6 green onions, roughly chopped

3 cloves garlic, roughly chopped

1 green bell pepper, roughly chopped

½ cup pumpkin seeds (pepitas), toasted

¼ cup sesame seeds, toasted

2 (8-inch) corn tortillas, torn into pieces

ECUADOR

- Put 6 cups water, tomatillos, chicken, jalapeños and salt into a large pot and bring to a boil.

- Reduce heat to medium low and simmer until tomatillos and jalapeño are tender and chicken is cooked through, about 25 minutes.

- Drain, reserving broth, and set aside chicken, tomatillos and jalapeños.

- Meanwhile, heat oil in a large skillet over medium heat.

- Add cilantro, green onions, garlic and bell pepper and cook until softened and golden brown, about 10 minutes; transfer to a blender.

- Add pumpkin seeds, sesame seeds, tortillas, 3 cups of the reserved broth, tomatillos and jalapeños (seeded first, if you like) and carefully purée until smooth; work in batches, if needed. (Reserve remaining broth for another use.)

- Transfer contents of the blender to a large pot and bring to a boil.

- Reduce heat to medium low and simmer until thickened, about 10 minutes.

- Meanwhile, discard bones from chicken and shred meat.

- Transfer to the pot with sauce and simmer 10 minutes more.

- Ladle into bowls, garnish with cilantro and serve.

Sulu Kofta

Top photo courtesy of Whole Foods Market's Ha Lam.
Bottom photo courtesy of Whole Planet Foundation's Brian Doe.

Ayse, Turkey

BUSINESS: small restaurant

Ayse (pronounced Aisha) is a microcredit client in Turkey where Whole Foods Market sources spices including cumin, oregano and fennel seed. Through Whole Planet Foundation's partner Turkish Grameen Microcredit Program, Ayse took a $500 loan and opened a small restaurant serving hot lunches of standard Turkish meals to workers in Denizli. Like her fellow group members borrowing from Turkish Grameen Microcredit Program, Ayse has worked hard with her loan and set up a small business that she manages with a friend and the occasional help of her two young daughters. Preparing traditional soups and stews, which are staples in this community, Ayse has managed to create an income that also lets her as a single mother watch her children when they are home from school. Learn more about Ayse and other entrepreneurs at *wholeplanetfoundation.org*.

SPICY LAMB AND POTATO SOUP

Whole Foods Market® tested recipe

SERVES 4

This soulful soup will give you an idea why **KOFTA** (made with spiced ground meat) is such a beloved dish in Turkey. In this recipe, savory lamb meatballs are served with tender potatoes and a host of vegetables in a simple broth. This recipe was inspired by Ayse, a microcredit client of Whole Planet Foundation's microfinance partner Turkish Grameen Microcredit Program.

¾ pound ground lamb

⅓ cup grated onion

¾ teaspoon ground allspice

¼ teaspoon ground black pepper

3 tablespoons finely chopped fresh parsley, divided

½ teaspoon fine sea salt, divided

5 cups low-sodium beef or vegetable broth

3 Russet potatoes (about 1½ pounds total), peeled and diced

2 carrots, diced

2 tablespoons tomato paste

Pinch cayenne pepper

⅔ cup frozen peas

- Preheat the oven to 425°F.

- In a large bowl, combine lamb, onion, allspice, pepper, 2 tablespoons of the parsley and ¼ teaspoon of the salt.

- Mix gently with your hands or a spatula until just combined.

- Form the mixture into meatballs about the size of large marbles (you should have about 30).

- Place meatballs on an oiled, large rimmed baking sheet and bake until just cooked through, 12 to 15 minutes, shaking the baking sheet once or twice during cooking.

- Meanwhile, in a large pot, combine broth, potatoes, carrots, tomato paste, cayenne and remaining ¼ teaspoon salt and bring to a boil.

- Lower heat and simmer, uncovered, until potatoes are very tender, about 20 minutes.

- Add meatballs along with any juices that accumulated on the baking sheet and peas to the pot and simmer a few more minutes.

- Serve garnished with remaining 1 tablespoon parsley.

TURKEY

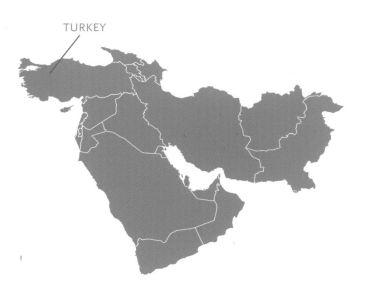

Mahluta Corbasi

Ayse, Turkey

BUSINESS: small restaurant

In addition to the recipe on page 43, here is another traditional Turkish recipe from Ayse's small restaurant *Tadim* (pictured on page 45), which is located in Denizli, an industrial town located six hours south of Istanbul. Ayse primarily serves workers from the town as the location is a great lunch spot, and *Lentil Soup* is a staple *Tadim* menu item, flavored with lemon and spices that are ubiquitous across Turkey and the Middle East. Being able to run home-based businesses or businesses near the home is one of the most common benefits clients mention when talking about the services offered by Turkish Grameen Microcredit Program. In an industrial town like Denizli, often the only other option is factory work which requires paying for child care and transport to work. Learn more about Ayse and other entrepreneurs at *wholeplanetfoundation.org*.

Top photo courtesy of Whole Foods Market's Ha Lam.
Bottom photo courtesy of Whole Planet Foundation's Brian Doe.

WHOLE PLANET
FOUNDATION

RED LENTIL SOUP

Whole Foods Market® tested recipe

(SERVES 6)

This version of Turkey's classic lentil soup is home cooking at its best: simple, flavorful and nutritious. Make it a complete meal by adding a tangy salad and your favorite flatbread or a crusty loaf of whole grain bread. This recipe was inspired by Ayse, a microcredit client of Whole Planet Foundation's microfinance partner Turkish Grameen Microcredit Program.

1⅓ cups (about 8 ounces) red lentils, picked through and rinsed

7 cups low-sodium vegetable broth

1 large onion, diced

1 large carrot, diced

4 cloves garlic, finely chopped

2 tablespoons tomato paste

1 teaspoon ground cumin

⅛ teaspoon cayenne pepper

¾ teaspoon fine sea salt

Lemon wedges and chopped mint for serving (optional)

- In a large pot, combine lentils, broth, onion, carrot, garlic, tomato paste, cumin and cayenne and bring to a boil over high heat.

- Lower heat and simmer, uncovered, until vegetables are very tender and lentils begin to fall apart, about 25 minutes.

- Remove the pot from the heat and use an immersion blender to quickly blend the soup until it is creamy but not completely puréed. Or, you can blend about half the soup in an upright blender, but use caution when blending hot liquids: blend only in small batches, hold the lid down firmly with a kitchen towel, and begin blending on low speed.

- Add salt and serve with lemon wedges and a garnish of mint if desired.

TURKEY

Photo courtesy of Whole Planet Foundation's Brian Doe.

Berbere Stew

Letegebrial, Ethiopia

BUSINESS: chickpea roasting

Letegebrial is a microcredit client in southern Oromia, Ethiopia where Whole Foods Market sources Whole Trade® coffee through Allegro Coffee Company®. Letegebrial is known as the best chickpea roaster in her village, where people struggle for food security, and she is the inspiration for *Ethiopian Chickpea Stew*. Whole Planet Foundation has granted $2 million for microfinance projects in Ethiopia, one of the poorest countries on Earth where four out of five people live on less than $2 a day. Isolation and lack of infrastructure are the prevailing conditions of life in rural Ethiopia. Through Whole Planet Foundation partners OCSSCO and A Glimmer of Hope, access to financial services will enable the poor to use their own hard work and creativity to lift themselves and their families out of poverty. Learn more about Letegebrial and other entrepreneurs at *wholeplanetfoundation.org*.

Top photo courtesy of Whole Foods Market's Ha Lam.
Bottom photo courtesy of A Glimmer of Hope.

WHOLE PLANET
FOUNDATION®

ETHIOPIAN-STYLE CHICKPEA STEW

Whole Foods Market® tested recipe

SERVES 6

Chickpea stews with flavors similar to this one are often made in Ethiopia using ground roasted chickpeas or even split peas. Here, the method is simplified but the stew's sweet, fragrant spice mixture, called **BERBERE**, remains. To save time, omit roasting the chickpeas and simply add them to the stew after they've been drained and rinsed. This recipe was inspired by Letegebrial, a microcredit client of Whole Planet Foundation's first microfinance partner OCSSCO via A Glimmer of Hope in Ethiopia.

1 teaspoon sweet paprika

1 teaspoon fine sea salt

½ teaspoon ground allspice

½ teaspoon ground black pepper

½ teaspoon ground cardamom

½ teaspoon ground cloves

½ teaspoon ground coriander

¼ to ½ teaspoon cayenne pepper

¼ teaspoon ground fenugreek (optional)

½ teaspoon ground ginger

2 (15-ounce) cans no-salt-added chickpeas, (also known as garbanzo beans) drained and rinsed

3 tablespoons extra-virgin olive oil, divided

2 cloves garlic, finely chopped

1 medium red onion, chopped

1 (1-inch) piece fresh ginger, peeled and finely chopped

1 (8-ounce) can no-salt-added tomato sauce

1 quart low-sodium vegetable broth

1 pound red potatoes, cut into 1-inch chunks

4 carrots, cut into 1-inch chunks

- Preheat the oven to 450°F. Stir together paprika, salt, allspice, black pepper, cardamom, cloves, coriander, cayenne, fenugreek (if using) and ginger in a small bowl; set spice mixture aside.

- Toss chickpeas with a tablespoon of the oil on a large rimmed baking sheet and spread out in a single layer.

- Roast chickpeas, stirring occasionally, until somewhat dried out and just golden brown, 16 to 18 minutes; set aside.

- Meanwhile, heat remaining 2 tablespoons oil in a medium pot over medium heat.

- Add garlic, onion and chopped ginger and cook, stirring occasionally, until very soft and golden brown, 8 to 10 minutes.

- Stir in spice mixture and continue cooking, stirring constantly, until spices are toasted and very fragrant, about 2 minutes.

- Stir in tomato sauce and cook 2 minutes more.

- Stir in broth, potatoes, carrots and roasted chickpeas and bring to a boil.

- Reduce heat to medium-low, cover and simmer until potatoes and carrots are just tender, about 20 minutes.

- Uncover the pot and simmer until stew is thickened and potatoes and carrots are very tender, about 25 minutes more.

- Ladle stew into bowls and serve.

ETHIOPIA

Sopa de Carne y Papa

Manuela, Peru

BUSINESS: fruit stand

Manuela is a microcredit client in Peru where Whole Foods Market sources quinoa and Whole Trade® bananas and mangoes. Through Whole Planet Foundation's partner Pro Mujer, poor women in Latin America are provided with the means to build livelihoods for themselves and futures for their families through microfinance, business training and health support. Manuela likes Pro Mujer, not just for the microcredit loans they offer but also for other services like their mobile health campaign. Whole Planet Foundation is proud to partner with Pro Mujer in Peru, Argentina, Bolivia, Mexico and Nicaragua. Learn more about Manuela and other entrepreneurs at *wholeplanetfoundation.org*.

Top photo courtesy of Whole Foods Market's Ha Lam.
Bottom photo courtesy of Sophie Eckrich.

WHOLE PLANET
FOUNDATION®

PERUVIAN BEEF AND POTATO SOUP

Whole Foods Market® tested recipe

SERVES 4

This soup is quick to prepare and delicious, too. To spice it up, add chopped fresh chiles before serving. This recipe was inspired by Manuela, a microcredit client of Whole Planet Foundation's microfinance partner Pro Mujer in Peru.

1 pound ground beef

1 yellow onion, chopped

1 red bell pepper, chopped

2 cloves garlic, finely chopped

3½ cups beef broth, preferably low-sodium

2 medium Yukon Gold potatoes, peeled and finely chopped

1 tablespoon ground cumin

1 bay leaf

¼ pound dried capellini pasta

Salt and pepper to taste

- Cook beef in a large pot over medium heat until browned and cooked through.

- Remove from the pot, set it aside and pour off all but 1 tablespoon of the fat.

- Add onion, bell pepper and garlic and cook over moderately high heat until softened, about 4 minutes.

- Add broth, 1 cup water, potatoes, cumin and bay leaf.

- Bring to a simmer and cook for 10 minutes.

- Add pasta and simmer until just tender, about 5 minutes.

- Return browned meat and cook until warmed through, about 1 minute.

- Discard bay leaf, taste and adjust seasoning with salt and pepper, and serve.

PERU

Githeri

Geoffrey, Kenya
BUSINESS: Field Officer

Geoffrey is a credit officer for Whole Planet Foundation's partner, One Acre Fund, in Kenya. Kenya is eligible for Whole Planet Foundation partnership because Whole Foods Market sources coffee through Allegro Coffee Company® throughout East Africa, including Kenya. However, One Acre Fund's work in Kenya is focused on small scale subsistence farming which is the dominant activity of the world's poor. In fact, One Acre Fund makes that activity twice as productive. Through credit officers like Geoffrey, One Acre Fund provides an $80 loan in the form of basic seed and fertilizer delivered within walking distance of the farmer, training on correct usage of farm inputs to improve farm profitability and knowledge to sell harvests at a significant profit. Credit officers work regularly with their clients, and most of One Acre Fund's staff are regular farmers themselves. Credit officers like Geoffrey are the unsung heroes of the microfinance industry, dedicated to empowering their community to lift itself out of poverty, second only to the hard work, creativity and ingenuity of the microcredit clients themselves. Learn more about Geoffrey and other heroes at *wholeplanetfoundation.org*.

Top photo courtesy of Whole Foods Market's Ha Lam.
Bottom photo courtesy of Whole Planet Foundation's Brian Doe.

KENYAN CORN AND BEAN STEW

Whole Foods Market® tested recipe

SERVES 4

This simple, nourishing stew originated with the Kikuyu tribe in Kenya. Today it is eaten throughout the country as a staple dish. This recipe was inspired by Geoffrey, a field officer of Whole Planet Foundation's microfinance partner One Acre Fund in Kenya.

1 cup dried kidney beans, soaked overnight or 2½ cups cooked kidney beans

1 tablespoon canola oil

1 yellow onion, chopped

3 tablespoons tomato paste

3 cups corn kernels, fresh (about 4 ears) or frozen

2 potatoes, cut into ½-inch cubes

¾ teaspoon fine sea salt

- If using dried beans, drain and place in a medium saucepot. Cover by 2 inches of water and bring to a boil.

- Reduce heat to a simmer and cook about 1 hour or until tender. Drain.

- In a large high-sided skillet or saucepot, heat oil over medium heat.

- Add onion and cook 10 minutes or until tender and golden, stirring occasionally.

- Stir in tomato paste and cook 1 minute, stirring.

- Add cooked beans, corn, potatoes, 4 cups water and salt and bring to a boil.

- Reduce heat to medium and simmer 25 minutes or until potatoes are tender and most liquid has been absorbed, stirring occasionally.

KENYA

Photo courtesy of Whole Planet Foundation's Brian Doe.

Kangkee Lek

Photos courtesy of Whole Planet Foundation's Daniel Zoltani.

Taunjai, Thailand
BUSINESS: silk weaver

Taunjai is a microcredit client in the Surin region of Thailand where Whole Foods Market sources rice through Alter Eco. Taunjai has been a silk weaver since childhood, learning from her mother before her parents died when she was still young. Through Whole Planet Foundation's partner Small Enterprise Development, Taunjai is on her eighth microcredit loan of $330, and as a proven entrepreneur, she now has the opportunity to borrow from commercial banks yet would need to use her house as collateral. Small Enterprise Development microloans are sufficient for her business and Taunjai wants only loan amounts she knows she can repay. With working capital from her loans, she purchases the raw silk thread to dye and weave into beautiful textiles, utilizing flowers, berries and minerals for color. To supplement household income, Taunjai and her family maintain a vegetable garden, orchard, chickens and ducks. Taunjai currently lives with her husband, his father, their two children and her sister. She is very proud to be the main moneymaker of the household, a value she reveres from growing up extremely poor. Learn more about Taunjai and other entrepreneurs at *wholeplanetfoundation.org*.

CURRY STEW

Whole Foods Market® tested recipe

(SERVES 8)

This coconut-curry stew with pork and bitter greens is pleasantly spicy, salty and sour. Make your own coconut milk using shredded coconut and hot water* or substitute canned coconut milk for equally delicious results. This recipe was inspired by Taunjai, a microcredit client of Whole Planet Foundation's microfinance partner Small Enterprise Development Company in Thailand.

1 teaspoon canola oil

½ small red onion, thinly sliced

1 (2½-pound) boneless pork loin roast, cut into very thin slices

8 dried red chiles

½ teaspoon fine sea salt

6 cloves garlic, finely chopped

2 dried Kaffir lime leaves

5 fresh lemongrass stalks, white part only, bruised

1 tablespoon bergamot zest or lime zest

½ teaspoon shrimp paste

1 (14-ounce) can coconut milk

1 tablespoon soy sauce

1½ teaspoons fish sauce

1 teaspoon sugar

1 cup boiled kee lek/cassia leaves and flowers, or 2 cups chopped bitter greens such as escarole, dandelion or mustard greens

Steamed jasmine rice for serving

- Heat oil in a large pot over medium heat.

- Add onion and cook, stirring occasionally, until translucent, 3 to 4 minutes.

- Working in batches, brown pork on both sides and set aside.

- Add chiles, salt, garlic, Kaffir lime leaves, lemongrass, lime zest and shrimp paste and stir to combine.

- Cook until fragrant, about 1 minute.

- Add coconut milk, soy sauce, fish sauce, sugar, ¼ cup water and reserved pork.

- Bring to a simmer and cook until the flavors are combined and pork is cooked through, about 15 minutes.

- Remove from heat and add kee lek or greens and stir to combine and warm through.

- Serve immediately over steamed rice.

* In a medium saucepan, bring 2 cups water to a boil. Add 3 cups unsweetened shredded coconut and stir to combine. Lower heat and simmer until water is absorbed, about 15 minutes. Remove from the heat and let cool. Transfer coconut mixture to a food processor or blender and purée until smooth. Strain through a fine mesh sieve or cheesecloth and discard remaining coconut.

THAILAND

Smalor Korko

Photos courtesy of Whole Planet Foundation's Daniel Zoltani.

Poul, Cambodia

BUSINESS: small restaurant

Poul is a microcredit client in Phnom Penh, Cambodia where Whole Foods Market sources handicrafts from Global Girlfriend. Poul lives with her husband and their three children and operates a small restaurant out of her family's two-bedroom home, which also houses eight other people. She is currently on her second loan cycle with Whole Planet Foundation's partner Chamroeun, utilizing the capital to purchase materials for the restaurant. Poul, who is 49, says she is still learning new cooking techniques at times, visiting the local market to get recipe ideas. Poul often spends most of the day preparing food, starting at five o'clock in the morning when she goes to the market and ending her day as late as nine o'clock in the evening. She sells her dishes from her kitchen and also delivers. Although Poul has plenty of customers who come to her home, she looks forward to going to the market and making deliveries for the change of atmosphere, as she is in the kitchen most of the day. She hopes one day to have a bigger restaurant space with tables and chairs so she can accommodate more customers. Learn more about Poul and other entrepreneurs at *wholeplanetfoundation.org*.

SPICY VEGETABLE SOUP

This spicy soup **SMALOR KORKO** is Poul's recipe and consists of papaya, citronella, pumpkin, bananas and toasted rice, prepared her way. Poul is a microcredit client of Whole Planet Foundation's microfinance partner Chamroeun Microfinance in Cambodia.

Pork rib or chicken

1 papaya

1 small ripe pumpkin

3 unripe bananas

Vegetables of choice

Citronella

Ginger

Saffron

Small sour orange skin or leaf

Garlic

Salt

Fish paste

Fish oil

Sugar

Toasted rice

- Cut the pork rib or chicken into small strips or cubes.

- Chop all vegetables into small cubes.

- Pound the citronella, saffron, ginger, small sour orange skin or leaf and garlic together until finely ground and completely mixed.

- Chop the fish paste until it is smooth and fine.

- Coat frying pan with oil, turn burner to a medium high temperature and add the fish paste and ground spices.

- Heat until mixture has a good aroma, then remove from heat.

- Place pork rib or chicken into a pot with water and boil for 10 minutes.

- Add chopped vegetables, add more water and let cook for 5 minutes.

- Add the toasted rice and mixture of citronella, saffron, ginger, garlic and sour orange skin or leaf.

- Combine additional ingredients of fish oil, salt, and sugar to taste.

- Simmer all ingredients for 1-2 minutes.

- Pour into a soup bowl and serve.

CAMBODIA

Journey with us from the United States to Mexico, Honduras and Nicaragua then south to Bolivia and Chile, over to Morocco, Senegal and Ghana, eastward to Tanzania, north to Israel, further east to India, Sri Lanka, Thailand, Cambodia and Vietnam, south to Indonesia, and further southeast to the islands of Fiji and Tonga with Brian Doe, Evan Lambert, Steve Wanta and Daniel Zoltani. Evan Lambert vacated his position as Whole Planet Foundation's Regional Director for Latin America in 2013 to relocate back to the United States with his wife and newborn daughter. Beforehand, he visited Mexico with Whole Planet Foundation's Global Programs Director Steve Wanta to monitor and evaluate Pro Mujer, our microfinance partner in Mexico and four other Latin American countries. One afternoon they had the pleasure of meeting microcredit client Josefina and her sister Patti who demonstrated how to make their popular **TAMALES**. Visit *wholeplanetfoundation.org* to see videos of Josefina and Patti in their kitchen along with Pro Mujer and Whole Planet Foundation staff. And, from all of us at Whole Planet Foundation, best wishes Evan!

Top left photo courtesy of Pro Mujer.

Top right photo courtesy of Whole Planet Foundation's Daniel Zoltani.

Bottom photo courtesy of Whole Planet Foundation's Evan Lambert.

Opposite Page: Photo courtesy of Small Enterprise Development.

ENTRÉES

Kanome Jiin Gang Keow Waan

Boonlam, Thailand

BUSINESS: catering

Boonlam is a microcredit client in the Surin region of Thailand where Whole Foods Market sources rice through Alter Eco. Whole Planet Foundation's partner Small Enterprise Development's vision is to alleviate poverty in low income and poor families of Thailand and empower women through a sustainable poverty-focused lending program. Thailand is in southeastern Asia, bordering the Andaman Sea and the Gulf of Thailand, southeast of Burma. A unified Thai kingdom was established in the mid-14th century, though it was known as Siam until 1939. It is slightly more than twice the size of Wyoming and has a population of nearly 70 million. Entrepreneurs like Boonlam have credit alternatives like borrowing from the Government Savings Bank, but the minimum loan size is prohibitively larger than she could utilize, and this type of loan does not provide the support and technical assistance of the village banking model provided by Small Enterprise Development. Learn more about Boonlam and other entrepreneurs at *wholeplanetfoundation.org*.

Top photo courtesy of Whole Foods Market's Ha Lam.
Bottom photo courtesy of Whole Planet Foundation's Daniel Zoltani.

WHOLE PLANET
FOUNDATION

GREEN CURRY CHICKEN WITH RICE VERMICELLI

Whole Foods Market® tested recipe

SERVES 4

Green curry paste and coconut milk make a flavorful base for this Thai curry featuring chicken, green beans and basil. Enjoy the colorful photo of the vermicelli Boonlam serves with this dish. This recipe was inspired by Boonlam, a microcredit client of Whole Planet Foundation's microfinance partner Small Enterprise Development Company in Thailand.

2 tablespoons canola oil

2 tablespoons prepared green curry paste

1 (14-ounce) can light coconut milk, divided

1 pound boneless, skinless chicken breast, cut into bite-size pieces

¾ pound green beans, trimmed and cut into 1-inch pieces

8 ounces pad thai or stir-fry rice vermicelli

2 tablespoons fish sauce

1 tablespoon sugar

½ cup fresh basil

1 red chile pepper, thinly sliced (optional)

- Heat oil in a large high-sided skillet over medium-high heat until hot but not smoking.

- Add curry paste and 1¼ cups coconut milk and whisk constantly until smooth.

- Bring to a boil, stirring to prevent scorching.

- Add chicken and green beans and return to a boil.

- Cook about 8 minutes or until chicken is cooked through and green beans are tender, stirring frequently.

- Meanwhile, prepare rice vermicelli according to package instructions.

- Add remaining coconut milk to the skillet and return to a boil.

- Stir in fish sauce, sugar and basil and remove from heat.

- Serve over rice vermicelli, garnished with chiles, if you like.

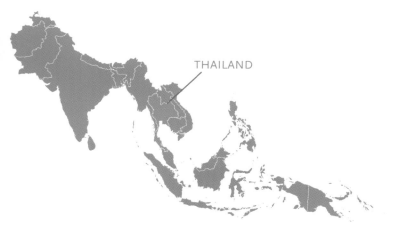

THAILAND

Photo courtesy of Whole Planet Foundation's Daniel Zoltani.

Kichuri

Anowara, Bangladesh

BUSINESS: fish farmer

Anowara is a fish farmer in the Rajshahi Division of northwest Bangladesh. Bangladesh is eligible for Whole Planet Foundation partnership because Whole Foods Market sells Teatulia Organic Teas whose single-source tea originates in northern Bangladesh. Anowara has been a microcredit client of Whole Planet Foundation's partner Grameen Motsho O Pashusampad Foundation for nearly 20 years. Due to the closing of the fisheries, Anowara has recently lost a significant portion of her income so she is being supported by her youngest son but struggles with this situation. Anowara says, *"I would like to return to work on the ponds. I enjoy keeping busy and would like the freedom of my own income."* Anowara, along with her neighbors, will continue to search for ways to return to fish farming. Learn more about Anowara and other entrepreneurs at *wholeplanetfoundation.org*.

Photos courtesy of Whole Planet Foundation's Daniel Zoltani.

WHOLE PLANET
FOUNDATION®

RICE AND LENTILS WITH CAULIFLOWER, PEAS AND ONIONS

Whole Foods Market® tested recipe

SERVES 6

Made with mung beans or lentils and rice, this traditional South Asian comfort food is known as **KICHURI**. If you prefer a dish with more heat, use serrano peppers instead of jalapeños. This recipe was inspired by Anowara, a microcredit client of Whole Planet Foundation's microfinance partner Grameen Motsho O Pashusampad Foundation in Bangladesh.

1¼ cups brown rice

2 cups lentils or split mung beans, toasted

½ teaspoon ground coriander

1 teaspoon ground ginger

½ teaspoon ground turmeric

2 teaspoons ground cumin

½ teaspoon sugar

1½ teaspoons fine sea salt

1 small cauliflower, broken into large florets

½ cup frozen peas, thawed

1 Russet potato, peeled and diced

½ cup frozen pearl onions, thawed

6 jalapeño or serrano peppers, cut lengthwise

2 tablespoons ghee

4 dried red chile peppers

4 bay leaves

1 cinnamon stick, broken in half

4 green cardamom pods

6 cloves

½ small onion, thinly sliced

- In a large pot, bring 6 cups water to a boil and add rice and beans.

- Lower heat and simmer for 15 minutes.

- Add coriander, ginger, turmeric, cumin, sugar and salt and stir to combine.

- Add cauliflower, peas, potato, pearl onions and peppers and stir well to combine.

- Cover and simmer until vegetables are tender and rice and beans are cooked through, 25 to 30 minutes.

- Meanwhile, melt ghee in a small skillet over medium-low heat.

- Add dried chile peppers, bay leaves, cinnamon stick, cardamom pods and cloves and cook for 2 to 3 minutes.

- Add sliced onion and cook, stirring occasionally, until golden brown, 5 to 7 minutes.

- Remove and discard chile peppers, bay leaves, cinnamon stick, cardamom pods and cloves.

- Stir ghee and onion mixture into cooked rice and beans.

- Serve immediately.

BANGLADESH

Egg Hoppers

Photos courtesy of Whole Planet Foundation's Daniel Zoltani.

Anoma, Sri Lanka

BUSINESS: bakery

Anoma is a microcredit client who lives with her husband an young son in the Gampaha District of Sri Lanka. Sri Lanka i eligible for Whole Planet Foundation partnership becaus Whole Foods Market sells Dr. Bronner's Fair Trade & Organi Coconut Oil that originates from that country. Anoma sells traditional dish named *Egg Hopper*, a recipe learned from he mother as a young girl. Using the front of her home as a baker to sell Egg Hoppers, she stays consistently busy saying, "thi is a daily hot selling item." She sells a daily average of abou 75 pieces priced individually at 30 LKR (Sri Lankan Rupee 23 cents) with egg and 10 LKR (8 cents) without egg Through Whole Planet Foundation's partner BRAC, Anom used a portion of her first loan to purchase a gas stove t replace the kerosene stove she was previously using. This cu down the cost of gas used and is a much more efficient wa to cook, she says. She plans to purchase a grinder with th second loan to be used to grind the rice into flour. Currentl she has to pay for this service. She has been doing thi daily business for five years now but recently has been abl to expand and improve the quality due to the microcred loans. Learn more about Anoma and other entrepreneurs a *wholeplanetfoundation.org*.

SRI LANKAN CRÊPES WITH EGGS

Whole Foods Market® tested recipe

SERVES 4

These crêpe-like "bowls" are a popular street food in Sri Lanka enjoyed sweet or savory for breakfast, lunch or dinner. Made from rice flour and coconut milk, the crisp hoppers form edible bowls for simply cooked eggs. Serve with a spicy chile sauce, chutney and fresh herbs. This recipe was inspired by Anoma, a microcredit client of Whole Planet Foundation's microfinance partner BRAC in Sri Lanka.

3 tablespoons warm water (about 110°F)

1 teaspoon active dry yeast

1½ cups rice flour

1 teaspoon sugar

½ teaspoon fine sea salt, divided

1 (14-ounce) can light coconut milk

4 eggs

- Place warm water in a small bowl and add yeast.
- Let yeast dissolve, about 5 minutes.
- Meanwhile, in a large bowl, combine flour, sugar and ¼ teaspoon of the salt.
- Add yeast mixture and coconut milk to flour mixture and whisk until blended.
- Cover and let rise 2 hours.
- Whisk to deflate.
- Heat an 8-inch non-stick skillet over medium heat.
- Add ½ cup batter and swirl to coat pan, including sides. Cook 1 minute to set.
- Crack egg in center. Cover skillet and cook 2 to 3 minutes or until egg and hopper (crêpe) are cooked through.
- Sprinkle with a pinch of salt.
- Remove and repeat with remaining ingredients
- Serve immediately.

SRI LANKA

Photo courtesy of Whole Planet Foundation's Daniel Zoltani.

Gallo Pinto

Maria, Nicaragua

BUSINESS: street food vendor

Maria is a microcredit client in the Estelí region of Nicaragua where Whole Foods Market sources Whole Trade® coffee through Allegro Coffee Company®. She caters out of her house, so her main activity is a *fritanga*—a Nicaraguan custom of selling homemade, street-side meals to go. Every evening, Maria sets up a table full of food, and hungry neighbors swarm, many taking food home to their families. Through Whole Planet Foundation's partner Pro Mujer, Maria has invested her loans in her house, improving the working conditions of her home-based business as well as living conditions for her family. She has replaced her wooden roof with a tin roof, tiled her once dirt floors and added on two rooms. Maria is embarking on her seventeenth loan cycle. Over the course of eight years, she has used loans to develop her business which has grown to provide jobs for 10 women. Learn more about Maria and other entrepreneurs at *wholeplanetfoundation.org*.

Photos courtesy of Whole Foods Market's Ha Lam.

WHOLE PLANET
FOUNDATION®

RICE AND BEANS

Whole Foods Market® tested recipe

(SERVES 6)

GALLO PINTO, or "spotted rooster," gets its name from the black or red beans and their dark liquid that speckle the rice. This national dish of Costa Rica and Nicaragua, served alongside fried eggs, meat or plantains, is often flavored with Salsa Lizano, a beloved vegetable-based condiment. In the United States, Worcestershire sauce is a close substitute. This recipe was inspired by Maria, a microcredit client of Whole Planet Foundation's microfinance partner Pro Mujer in Nicaragua.

4 tablespoons canola oil, divided

2 cups uncooked long grain white rice

6 tablespoons chopped fresh cilantro, divided

2 cloves garlic, finely chopped

1 small yellow onion, chopped

½ red bell pepper, chopped

Salt and ground black pepper to taste

2 (15-ounce) cans black beans, drained, liquid reserved

1 tablespoon Worcestershire sauce (optional)

- Heat 1 tablespoon of the oil in a medium pot over medium high heat.

- Add rice and cook, stirring often, until opaque, about 2 minutes.

- Add 3 cups water and salt, then reduce heat to medium low.

- Cover the pot and simmer, without uncovering or stirring, until rice is almost tender and liquid is just absorbed, about 15 minutes.

- Remove the pot from the heat and set aside for 5 minutes, then uncover and fluff rice with a fork. Set aside.

- Heat remaining 3 tablespoons oil in a large skillet over medium high heat.

- Add 2 tablespoons of the cilantro, garlic, onion, bell pepper, salt and pepper and stir well.

- Cook, stirring often, until golden brown, 8 to 10 minutes.

- Add reserved rice, beans and ⅓ cup of the reserved bean liquid (discard remaining liquid) and Worcestershire sauce.

- Stir gently to coat, and cook, stirring occasionally, until hot throughout, 2 to 3 minutes more.

- Stir in remaining cilantro and season with salt and pepper.

- Transfer rice and beans to bowls and serve, topped with a fried egg or a dollop of sour cream, if you like.

NICARAGUA

Chha Puos Tan Spei Chou

Leng, Cambodia

BUSINESS: small restaurant

Leng is a microcredit client in Phnom Penh where Whole Foods Market sources handicrafts through Global Girlfriend. Through Whole Planet Foundation's partner Chamroeun Microfinance, Leng has owned the same restaurant for five years, where she cooks and serves traditional dishes of Cambodia. Leng has been a borrower from Chamroeun for three consecutive years. See Leng's recipe for Salted Fish and Ground Pork Omelet (*Trei Proma Jien Poong Muern*) on page 85, and learn more about Leng and other entrepreneurs at *wholeplanetfoundation.org*.

Top photo courtesy of Whole Foods Market's Ha Lam.
Bottom photo courtesy of Whole Planet Foundation's Daniel Zoltani.

WHOLE PLANET
FOUNDATION

CAMBODIAN COLLARD GREENS WITH PORK BELLY

Whole Foods Market® tested recipe

$$\text{SERVES 4}$$

Collards cooked with diced pork belly make a hearty dish rich in flavor. This recipe was inspired by Leng, a microcredit client of Whole Planet Foundation's microfinance partner Chamroeun Microfinance in Cambodia.

1 tablespoon canola oil

4 ounces pork belly, cut into ¼-inch pieces

2 cloves garlic, minced

8 ounces mushrooms, coarsely chopped

2 tablespoons fish sauce

2 bunches collard greens, thick stems removed and leaves cut into 1-inch wide strips

¾ teaspoon sugar

- In a large skillet, heat oil over medium heat.
- Add pork belly and garlic; cook 3 minutes or until garlic is browned, stirring frequently.
- Stir in mushrooms and fish sauce.
- Reduce heat to medium-low, cover and cook 3 minutes or until mushrooms release liquid.
- Stir in greens, cover and cook 5 minutes or until beginning to wilt, stirring occasionally.
- Uncover and cook over medium-high heat 8 to 10 minutes, or until greens are tender and most of the liquid evaporates.
- Stir in sugar.

CAMBODIA

Pastel de Choclo

Marta, Chile

BUSINESS: neighborhood catering

Marta is a microcredit client in the Temuco region of southern Chile where Whole Foods Market sources blueberries. With support from Whole Planet Foundation's partner Fundación Banigualdad, Marta is known in her neighborhood for selling a delicious corn casserole dish. She lets her neighbors know when she will be preparing it, about every 10 days, and people can also order it for special occasions. Her dream is to be her own boss since she feels she is a savvy businesswoman. She knows how to break down the costs of items she sells like marmalade and casserole dishes, exactly how much she spent, the cost of her labor and the amount of her profit. Learn more about Marta and other entrepreneurs at *wholeplanetfoundation.org*.

Photos courtesy of Whole Planet Foundation's Evan Lambert.

CHILEAN BEEF AND CORN CASSEROLE

Whole Foods Market® tested recipe

(SERVES 6)

Inspired by the Chilean casserole, **PASTEL DE CHOCLO**, this dish combines spiced beef and tender onions and is topped with a creamy corn and basil mixture. This recipe was inspired by Marta, a microcredit client of Whole Planet Foundation's microfinance partner Fundación Banigualdad in Chile.

3 cups corn kernels

1 cup milk

½ cup heavy cream

¼ cup fresh basil

½ teaspoon coarse sea salt, divided

½ cup raisins

1 tablespoon canola oil

1 pound top sirloin beef, trimmed and cut into 1-inch cubes

1 teaspoon ground cumin

1 large onion, chopped

1 carrot, chopped

2 eggs, hard-cooked, peeled and chopped

- Combine corn, milk, cream, basil and ¼ teaspoon of the salt in a blender and process just until lightly blended.

- Transfer mixture to a medium saucepan and bring to a boil over medium-high heat.

- Reduce heat to medium and simmer about 12 minutes or until thickened, stirring occasionally.

- Soak raisins in hot water 10 minutes. Drain well.

- Meanwhile, in a large skillet, heat oil over medium-high heat.

- Add beef, cumin and remaining ¼ teaspoon salt and cook until browned, about 5 minutes.

- Remove with a slotted spoon to a paper-towel-lined plate.

- Add onion and carrot to the skillet and cook about 10 minutes or until browned and tender, adding ¼ cup water halfway through cooking and stirring occasionally to release the browned bits.

- Preheat the oven to 400°F.

- Spread beef in an 8x8-inch baking dish. Top with onion mixture, eggs and raisins.

- Pour corn batter on top and spread evenly.

- Bake 25 minutes.

- Increase oven temperature to broil and broil about 5 minutes or until top is golden brown.

CHILE

Chiles Rellenos

Martha
Chile Relleno
+ Picadillo
Ground Meat
Onion
Tomato
Pear
Apple
Garlic
Potato
+ Chile Poblano
+ White Whip
Add yolk
+ Grill
+ then Plastic
bag
+ w/ wet towel

Top photos courtesy of Whole Planet Foundation's Steve Wanta.
Recipe list courtesy of microcredit client Martha.
Bottom photo courtesy of Grameen America.

Martha, USA

BUSINESS: making and selling tamales

Martha is a microcredit client in Omaha, Nebraska where Whole Foods Market sources local products. Through a partnership with Grameen America, Whole Planet Foundation is empowering businesswomen like Martha in Austin, Texas; Boston, Massachusetts; Charlotte, North Carolina; Indianapolis, Indiana; Los Angeles, California; New York City, New York; Oakland, California; Omaha, Nebraska; San Juan, Puerto Rico and San Jose, California. Whole Planet Foundation has granted $4 million in the United States to empower women entrepreneurs with the opportunity to create or expand a business and lift themselves and their families out of poverty. Learn more about Martha and other entrepreneurs at *wholeplanetfoundation.org*.

WHOLE PLANET
FOUNDATION®

STUFFED PEPPERS

Whole Foods Market® tested recipe

SERVES 4

This version of **Chiles Rellenos** is baked instead of fried and maintains a fluffy batter-like coating. Shredded pear, an unorthodox addition to the filling, adds a touch of sweetness. This recipe was inspired by Martha, a microcredit client of Whole Planet Foundation's microfinance partner Grameen America in the United States.

4 large poblano chiles

1 tablespoon canola oil,
   plus more for the baking dish

½ cup chopped onion

2 cloves garlic, minced

½ pound ground beef

1 pear, peeled and shredded

1 tomato, chopped

¾ cup crumbled queso fresco

4 eggs, separated

½ teaspoon coarse sea salt

- To roast peppers, preheat the broiler. Place peppers on a broiler pan and cook about 2 inches from the heat source, turning once each side has blackened.

- Place in a large bowl and cover. Let peppers cool 10 minutes (to allow for easier skin removal).

- Remove skins from peppers. Make a slit on one side of each pepper and remove seeds and stem. Set aside until ready to stuff.

- Adjust the oven temperature to 400°F. Lightly oil an 8x8-inch glass or ceramic baking dish.

- Meanwhile, in a large skillet, heat oil over medium-high heat. Add onion and garlic and cook 6 to 8 minutes or until browned.

- Stir in beef, pear and tomato and cook 6 to 8 minutes longer, stirring occasionally, until beef is browned and mixture has thickened.

- Remove from heat and stir in queso fresco.

- Stuff peppers with beef mixture. Place stuffed peppers in the prepared baking dish.

- Place egg whites in a large bowl and beat with an electric mixture until stiff peaks form.

- Place egg yolks and salt in a separate small bowl and whisk until blended. Gently fold egg yolk mixture into egg whites until blended, being careful not to deflate egg whites.

- Spread egg mixture evenly around and on top of peppers in baking dish. Bake 30 minutes or until browned and crisp.

UNITED STATES

Yassadienne

Adama, Senegal

BUSINESS: restaurant

Adama is a microcredit client in the Kaolack region of Senegal where Whole Foods Market sources hibiscus juice. Kaolack sits at a crossroads between Gambia and the roads to Mali and Mauritania making it a prime location for small trade and commerce. Many women are becoming leaders in regional import and export of goods from neighboring areas thanks to access to microcredit from Whole Planet Foundation's partner CAURIE Microfinance. Adama runs a small restaurant outside of Kaolack and is in her third loan cycle with CAURIE Microfinance. Adama prepares typical dishes, like *Thieboudienne* (rice and fish) and *Yassadienne*. Learn more about Adama and other entrepreneurs at *wholeplanetfoundation.org*.

Photos courtesy of Whole Planet Foundation's Genie Bolduc.

WHOLE PLANET
FOUNDATION®

LEMON-MARINATED FISH WITH ONIONS AND CARROTS

Whole Foods Market® tested recipe

SERVES 4

Inspired by a dish in Senegal often made with chicken, this recipe uses tender fish fillets that are topped with a lemony carrot and onion mixture. Serve YASSADIENNE with plenty of couscous or try brown rice or quinoa. This recipe was inspired by Adama, a microcredit client of Whole Planet Foundation's microfinance partner CAURIE Microfinance in Senegal.

¾ cup lemon juice

½ cup plus 1 tablespoon canola oil, divided

½ cup chopped fresh parsley

3 bay leaves, crushed

1 teaspoon grated lemon zest

1 teaspoon fresh thyme leaves

1 teaspoon coarse sea salt

½ teaspoon ground black pepper

4 skinless, boneless fillets white fish, such as snapper or Chilean sea bass (about 1½ pounds total)

1 large onion, thinly sliced

2 large carrots, shredded

1 cup couscous

SENEGAL

- Combine lemon juice, ½ cup of the oil, parsley, bay leaves, lemon zest, thyme, salt and pepper in a wide shallow dish.

- Add fish and let marinate 2 hours, turning fish over halfway through marinating.

- In a large skillet, heat remaining 1 tablespoon oil.

- Remove fish from marinade and place in the hot skillet.

- Add onions and carrots to marinade.

- Cook fish just until browned on each side, about 3 minutes per side and remove to a plate.

- Remove onion mixture from marinade and cook over medium-high heat about 10 minutes or until browned. Discard remaining marinade.

- Add fish back to the skillet, cover with onions and carrots and cook 3 to 5 minutes or until fish is cooked through.

- Meanwhile, in a small pot, bring 1 cup water to a boil.

- Place couscous in a heat-proof medium bowl; pour boiling water over it and stir with a fork to combine.

- Cover and let stand for 10 minutes, then uncover and fluff with a fork.

- Serve fish and vegetables over couscous.

Thieboudienne

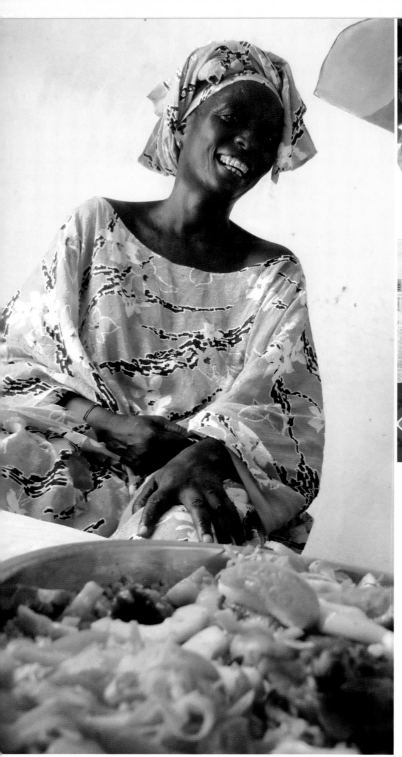

Left photo courtesy of Whole Planet Foundation's Steve Wanta.
Right photo courtesy of Whole Planet Foundation's Brian Doe.

Astou, Senegal

BUSINESS: restaurant

Astou is a microcredit client in Senegal where Whole Foods Market sources hibiscus juice. Astou is a married woman and mother with five children. Through Whole Planet Foundation's partner CAURIE Microfinance, Astou manages a restaurant in her neighborhood of Darou Salam, situated in the heart of Ndoffane. She typically prepares *Ndambé* (a meal of beans and tomato sauce) or *Thieboudienne* (Senegalese national dish of fish filled with local spices, slow cooked in vegetables and a tomato sauce) for lunch and *ragout* (a vegetable stew) or *touffé* (chicken cooked in a sauce of onions) for dinner. She also offers hot drinks like coffee and tea. Her clientele is made up of neighbors and travelers passing through Ndoffane, and also largely those who come to the weekly market (known as the *"Louma"*). Learn more about Astou and other entrepreneurs at *wholeplanetfoundation.org*.

WHOLE PLANET
FOUNDATION°

SENEGALESE RICE AND FISH

Whole Foods Market® tested recipe

SERVES 6

We used the traditional components of **THIEBOUDIENNE** (also known as **CEEBU JEN**), a dish from Senegal which translates into "rice and fish" in this hearty recipe. Fish fillets stuffed with an herb mixture are seared in peanut oil and then finish cooking atop a tomato vegetable stew. The fish and vegetables are served with rice seasoned with tomato broth from the stew. This recipe was inspired by Astou, a microcredit client of Whole Planet Foundation's microfinance partner CAURIE Microfinance in Senegal.

1½ cups long-grain white rice, thoroughly rinsed

3 tablespoons finely chopped fresh parsley

1 green onion, thinly sliced

2 cloves garlic, finely chopped

⅛ teaspoon fine sea salt

⅛ teaspoon cayenne pepper

6 (3-ounce) skinless, boneless portions halibut, sea bass or cod fillets

3 tablespoons peanut oil

1 medium yellow onion, chopped

2 carrots, diced

1 red bell pepper, diced

⅓ cup tomato paste

1 medium sweet potato, peeled and cut into ½-inch pieces

1½ cups diced eggplant

3 cups low-sodium chicken broth

1 (14.5-ounce) can diced tomatoes

- Place rice and 3 cups water in a medium saucepot and bring to a boil over medium-high heat. Reduce heat to medium-low, cover the pot and simmer until liquid is completely absorbed and rice is just tender, about 15 to 20 minutes. Set the covered pot aside off the heat for 10 minutes, then uncover and fluff rice with a fork.

- Meanwhile, in a small bowl, combine parsley, green onion, garlic, salt and cayenne.

- Cut 2 deep slits in each fish fillet and stuff with parsley mixture.

- In a large wide saucepot or Dutch oven, heat oil over medium heat until hot.

- Add fish and brown on both sides, about 5 minutes per side. Transfer to a plate and cover to keep warm.

- Add onion, carrots and bell pepper to the pot and cook 10 minutes or until tender, stirring occasionally.

- Stir in tomato paste and cook 1 minute.

- Add sweet potato, eggplant, broth and tomatoes and bring to a boil over medium-high heat.

- Reduce heat to medium and simmer until vegetables are tender, about 20 minutes.

- Carefully remove 1 cup liquid from saucepot and stir into rice.

- Place fish on top of vegetable mixture, cover and cook 3 to 5 minutes longer or until fish is cooked through and very hot.

- Spoon rice and vegetable mixture into serving bowls and top each with a piece of fish.

SENEGAL

Vegetable Tagine and Couscous

Top photo courtesy of Whole Foods Market's Ha Lam.
Bottom photo courtesy of Whole Planet Foundation's Genie Bolduc.

Habiba, Morocco

BUSINESS: innkeeper

Habiba is a microcredit client in Morocco where Whole Foods Market sources spices and essential oils through Frontier Co-op®. In the village of Tazantout, Habiba offers rooms in her house to rent to tourists. Through Whole Planet Foundation's partner INMAA, Habiba is on her seventh loan, utilizing the capital to make home improvements to provide a better experience to her clients. The profit from her business has helped her buy tables and other furniture and partially start a second house which will be for herself and her family so they can have their own home. The guesthouse is a full board experience, in which guests can lodge and enjoy meals prepared by Habiba and her staff. Typically the guests prefer the different Moroccan tagines, brochettes (grilled meats) and couscous dishes. She said her family's favorite meals are usually the tagines, with meat and vegetables. Habiba is hopeful about the future, and when she thinks about five years in the future, she hopes that she can keep her children's education on track. Learn more about Habiba and other entrepreneurs at *wholeplanetfoundation.org*.

MOROCCAN LEMON COUSCOUS WITH VEGETABLES

Whole Foods Market® tested recipe

SERVES 4

Named after the vessels they're traditionally cooked in, **TAGINES** often feature less-utilized cuts of meat that are stewed for a long time. This version is vegetable-based and cooks quite quickly. Its warm flavors pair wonderfully with a quick tart lemon couscous. This recipe was inspired by Habiba, a microcredit client of Whole Planet Foundation's microfinance partner INMAA in Morocco.

½ teaspoon ground cumin

½ teaspoon ground ginger

½ teaspoon ground turmeric

¼ teaspoon ground cinnamon

½ teaspoon fine sea salt

¼ teaspoon ground black pepper

2 tablespoons extra-virgin olive oil

1 yellow onion, chopped

3 cloves garlic, minced

2 tablespoons tomato paste

3 cups low-sodium vegetable or chicken broth

2 large sweet potatoes (about 1½ pounds), peeled and cut into ½-inch cubes

1 (14.5-ounce) can diced tomatoes

1 (15-ounce) can chickpeas (also known as garbanzo beans), drained and rinsed

½ cup raisins, preferably golden

¼ cup lemon juice

2 teaspoons grated lemon zest

1½ cups couscous

¼ cup chopped fresh parsley

- Combine cumin, ginger, turmeric, cinnamon, salt and pepper. Set aside.

- In a large high-sided skillet, heat oil over medium heat.

- Add onion and garlic; cook 8 to 10 minutes or until golden and tender.

- Stir in spice mixture and tomato paste and cook 1 minute, stirring.

- Stir in broth, potatoes, tomatoes and their juice, beans and raisins. Bring to a boil.

- Reduce heat to medium-low and simmer, covered, about 20 minutes or until potatoes are tender and sauce is thickened.

- Meanwhile, in a medium saucepan, bring 1½ cups water, lemon juice and zest to a boil.

- Remove from heat. Stir in couscous. Cover and let sit 5 minutes or until all liquid is absorbed.

- Fluff with a fork.

- Serve with vegetables and garnish with parsley.

MOROCCO

Photo courtesy of Whole Planet Foundation's Genie Bolduc.

Vegetarian Biryani

Bindu, India

BUSINESS: stationery shop and kiosk

Bindu is a microcredit client in Kerala, India where Whole Foods Market sources cashews, a local ingredient of *Vegetable Biryani*. Through Microcredit Initiative of Grameen, Whole Planet Foundation's first partner in India, Bindu started her stationery shop and kiosk with her first loan. She has invested subsequent loans in purchasing more goods to sell to grow her business, increasing volume and profit. Her dream is for her family to have a good house as well as education and a better future for herself and her two children. Learn more about Bindu and other entrepreneurs at *wholeplanetfoundation.org*.

Top photo courtesy of Whole Foods Market's Ha Lam.
Bottom photo courtesy of Whole Planet Foundation's Evan Lambert.

WHOLE PLANET
FOUNDATION®

INDIAN VEGETABLE RICE WITH CASHEWS

Whole Foods Market® tested recipe

SERVES 6-8

Top the finished **BIRYANI** with a fragrant mix of sliced jalapenos, tomato wedges and chopped cilantro, if you like. This recipe was inspired by Bindu, a microcredit client of Microcredit Initiative of Grameen, Whole Planet Foundation's first microfinance partner in India.

1 cup brown basmati rice, thoroughly rinsed

1 tablespoon canola oil

2 to 3 cloves garlic, chopped

1 large red onion, cut into thin wedges

1 (2-inch) piece ginger, peeled and finely chopped

½ cup chopped roasted cashews, divided

½ teaspoon fine sea salt, divided

½ teaspoon ground black pepper, divided

½ cup nonfat plain yogurt

1 tablespoon curry powder

5 cups chopped fresh vegetables, such as cauliflower, carrots or green beans

1 cup frozen peas

- Preheat the oven to 350°F. Bring a medium pot of water to a boil. Add rice and simmer for 30 minutes; drain well.

- Meanwhile, heat oil in a large ovenproof pot over medium high heat.

- Add garlic, onion, ginger, half of the cashews, ¼ teaspoon of the salt and ¼ teaspoon of the pepper. Cook, stirring often and adding a splash of water when the mixture sticks to the bottom of the pot, until deep golden brown and soft, about 15 minutes.

- Add yogurt and curry powder and cook until thickened, 2 to 3 minutes more.

- Stir in vegetables, ⅔ cup water, remaining ¼ teaspoon salt and ¼ teaspoon pepper, cover and simmer until vegetables are tender on the outside but not cooked through, about 5 minutes.

- Remove the pot from heat and stir in frozen peas.

- Arrange hot, drained rice over vegetables, cover the pot with foil and a tight-fitting lid and bake until rice and vegetables are tender, about 25 minutes.

- Uncover, carefully transfer contents of the pot to a large bowl and toss together gently. Spoon into bowls and serve garnished with remaining cashews.

INDIA

Rau Muống Ngâm Dấm Đường

Pham, Vietnam

BUSINESS: restaurant

Pham is a microcredit client in northeastern Vietnam where Whole Foods Market sources organic cinnamon through Frontier Co-op®. Pham has been a borrower of Whole Planet Foundation's partner Tao Yeu Mai for three consecutive years, using the funds to purchase supplies for her restaurant. Pham has owned and operated the same restaurant out of her home for 10 years. The family depends on the income generated from her business as well as that from her husband's job as a factory guard. She cooks everyday from 4:30 a.m. to 9 o'clock p.m. receiving a daily profit of 90,000 to 100,000 Vietnamese Dong, which is just under $5 USD. She has future aspirations to upgrade her restaurant and home and is currently saving money to do so. Learn more about Pham and other entrepreneurs at *wholeplanetfoundation.org*.

Photos courtesy of Whole Planet Foundation's Daniel Zoltani.

WHOLE PLANET
FOUNDATION®

VIETNAMESE PICKLED SPINACH WITH PORK OVER RICE

Whole Foods Market® tested recipe

SERVES 4

This recipe combines the tangy flavor of quick-pickled spinach with ground pork and is served over rice. The original version would use water spinach, but we substituted more widely available baby spinach. This recipe was inspired by Pham, a microcredit client of Whole Planet Foundation's microfinance partner Tao Yeu Mai in Vietnam.

½ cup white vinegar

½ teaspoon fine sea salt

8 cups packed baby spinach leaves

2 tablespoons canola oil

½ yellow onion, thinly sliced

2 cloves garlic, thinly sliced

1 pound lean ground pork

¼ teaspoon crushed red chile flakes

2 cups cooked long-grain white rice, for serving

- Place vinegar, salt and spinach in a large bowl and let sit 1 hour, tossing frequently, until spinach wilts.

- In a large skillet, heat oil over medium heat.

- Add onion and garlic; cook 6 minutes or until tender and golden, stirring occasionally.

- Add pork and chile flakes; cook 2 minutes, stirring constantly.

- Stir in spinach and vinegar mixture; continue to cook 5 to 7 minutes more or until pork is cooked through, stirring to release browned bits from the pan.

- Serve over rice.

VIETNAM

Photo courtesy of Whole Planet Foundation's Daniel Zoltani.

Red-Red

Regina, Ghana

BUSINESS: street food vendor

Regina is a microcredit client in the northern region of Ghana where Whole Foods Market sources baskets through The Blessing Basket Project and Alaffia. Ten years ago, Regina started her *Red-Red* business with an initial loan of $21 from her husband with which she purchased three bunches of plantains to make an average daily sale of $4, but the daily profit of 75 cents was too small to sustain her family. Sometimes the market would run out of product and Regina would have to wait until the market women returned from the south with fresh plantains. These business challenges continued until Regina joined Whole Planet Foundation's partner Grameen Ghana last year, as a member of the Wuni Songmiti credit group with an initial loan of $100. After repaying on time, Regina took advantage of a second loan for $300 and education provided by Grameen Ghana. Regina's profit increased and she added a new product, plantain chips. The chips are fried, dried and can be stored for long periods so Regina is able to sell them to shops and offices. Learn more about Regina and other entrepreneurs at *wholeplanetfoundation.org*.

Top photo courtesy of Whole Foods Market's Ha Lam.
Bottom photo courtesy of Whole Planet Foundation's Brian Doe.

WHOLE PLANET FOUNDATION

BLACK-EYED PEAS AND TOMATOES WITH SAUTÉED BANANAS

Whole Foods Market® tested recipe

SERVES 4

Inspired by the dish **RED-RED** from Ghana, this simple stew of tomatoes and black-eyed peas is traditionally served with fried plantains. Cooked bananas are a great substitute and the flavor combination, while surprising, is tasty and balanced. This recipe was inspired by Regina, a microcredit client of Whole Planet Foundation's microfinance partner Grameen Ghana.

1 tablespoon canola oil
1 onion, thinly sliced
1 clove garlic, finely chopped
½ teaspoon grated fresh ginger
⅛ teaspoon cayenne pepper
1 (28-ounce) can crushed tomatoes
1 (15-ounce) can black-eyed peas, drained and rinsed
¼ teaspoon fine sea salt
1 tablespoon unsalted butter
2 firm bananas, halved lengthwise and cut into chunks

- Heat oil in a large high-sided skillet over medium heat.
- Add onion and cook about 10 minutes or until golden and tender, stirring frequently.
- Stir in garlic, ginger and cayenne and cook for 1 minute, stirring constantly.
- Add tomatoes and peas and bring to a simmer.
- Cook 15 minutes or until peas are tender. Stir in salt.
- Meanwhile, melt butter in a separate skillet over medium-high heat.
- Reduce heat to medium, add bananas and cook about 5 minutes or until browned on both sides, gently flipping halfway through cooking.
- Serve alongside black-eyed peas in a shallow bowl.

GHANA

Photo courtesy of Whole Planet Foundation's Brian Doe.

Trei Proma Jien Poong Muern

Photos courtesy of Whole Planet Foundation's Daniel Zoltani.

Leng, Cambodia

BUSINESS: small restaurant

Leng is a microcredit client in Phnom Penh where Whole Foods Market sources handicrafts through Global Girlfriend. Through Whole Planet Foundation's partner Chamroeun Microfinance, Leng receives capital to run her restaurant featuring typical local cuisine like Cambodian Collard Greens with Pork Belly (*Chha Puos Tan Spei Chou*) on page 67. Chamroeun Microfinance is a microfinance organization active in Cambodia since 2006. Chamroeun's mission is to accompany families in urban depressed areas to develop long-term projects and increase their incomes by offering savings, loans and micro insurance services. Chamroeun helps people running small economic activities overcome unexpected expenses and improve their business skills and self confidence through trainings and business follow up. Learn more about Leng and other entrepreneurs at *wholeplanetfoundation.org*.

WHOLE PLANET
FOUNDATION

SALTED FISH AND GROUND PORK OMELET

Whole Foods Market® tested recipe

SERVES 2

Salted dried fish is a popular ingredient for omelets in Cambodia, and this delicious dish known as **TREI PROMA JIEN POONG MUERN** mixes it with ground pork. Be sure to start this recipe several days in advance to allow the salt cod to soften. This recipe was inspired by Leng, a microcredit client of Whole Planet Foundation's microfinance partner Chamroeun Microfinance in Cambodia.

Small piece (about 8 ounces) dried salt cod
⅓ cup (about 2½ ounces) ground pork
2 eggs
¼ cup finely chopped onion
1 clove garlic, minced
2 tablespoons vegetable broth or water
½ teaspoon sugar
¼ teaspoon ground black pepper
2 tablespoons fish sauce, divided
2 teaspoons canola oil
4 to 5 lettuce leaves
1 mango, diced
1 small cucumber, peeled and sliced
½ green bell pepper, diced
Juice of 1 lime

CAMBODIA

- Rinse salt cod thoroughly, place in a container and pour in enough cold water to cover by 2 inches.
- Cover and refrigerate, changing water 2 or 3 times a day, until fish is softened and no longer tastes overpoweringly salty, 1 to 2 days.
- Flake or dice enough fish to measure ⅓ cup; save the remainder for another use (it's excellent in soup).
- Place cod in a medium bowl and add pork; stir until mixed.
- Add eggs, onion, garlic, broth, sugar, black pepper and 1 tablespoon of the fish sauce, and whisk again.
- Heat oil in a medium skillet over medium heat.
- When hot, pour in egg mixture, cover the skillet and cook until the bottom is very brown, about 5 minutes, lifting edges with a rubber spatula occasionally and tilting the pan to let uncooked egg run underneath.
- Preheat the broiler.
- Place the skillet under the broiler and cook until pork is cooked through and egg is set and browned on top, 2 to 3 minutes.
- Line a platter with lettuce leaves.
- Loosen omelet around edges and bottom with a spatula and slide or invert onto the platter.
- Meanwhile, toss mango, cucumber and bell pepper with lime juice and remaining 1 tablespoon fish sauce. Serve with omelet.

Masam Jing

Zubaidah, Indonesia
BUSINESS: local restaurant

Zubaidah is a microcredit client in Sumatra, Indonesia where Whole Foods Market sources Whole Trade® coffee through Allegro Coffee Company®. Zubaidah is an entrepreneur from Takengon where she has owned and operated a local restaurant for the past six years. Currently on her third loan of $327 from Whole Planet Foundation's partner KOMIDA, Zubaidah is thankful for the availability of microfinance loans. She says the loans allow her to purchase the needed ingredients and materials to effectively operate her restaurant so that she can continue to successfully repay the weekly amounts. She qualifies for local bank loans but says the interest rates are too high and the collateral requirements too burdensome. Since becoming a microcredit client, Zubaidah has encouraged other women to also take advantage of the services provided. She is now proudly Center Chief, a leadership role that enables her to motivate her fellow borrowers and hold them accountable. Learn more about Zubaidah and other entrepreneurs at *wholeplanetfoundation.org*.

Top photo courtesy of Whole Foods Market's Ha Lam.
Bottom photo courtesy of Whole Planet Foundation's Daniel Zoltani.

INDONESIAN-STYLE FISH WITH TAMARIND-TURMERIC SAUCE

Whole Foods Market® tested recipe

SERVES 4

Tamarind and turmeric give a warm, tangy flavor, and coconut milk adds richness to this vibrant sauce for fish. This **MASAM JING** recipe is inspired by Zubaidah, a microcredit client of Whole Planet Foundation's microfinance partner KOMIDA in Indonesia, prepared her way.

1 tablespoon canola oil

1 yellow onion, coarsely chopped

2 cloves garlic, minced

1 teaspoon fine sea salt

1 teaspoon ground turmeric

¼ teaspoon crushed red chile flakes

4 teaspoons tamarind paste

½ cup coconut milk

1 (8-ounce) can bamboo shoots, drained

4 (6-ounce) fillets red snapper, grouper, rockfish or barramundi, skin on

⅓ cup fresh basil, thinly sliced

- In a large skillet or wok, heat oil over medium heat.
- Add onion, garlic and salt; cook until very tender, 6 to 7 minutes.
- Stir in turmeric and chile flakes and cook, stirring, 30 seconds.
- Meanwhile, dissolve tamarind paste in 1 cup hot water.
- Strain out and discard any seeds or stems.
- Add liquid to the skillet.
- Carefully transfer mixture to a blender and pulse until just chopped.
- Return to the skillet. Add coconut milk and bamboo shoots and bring to a boil.
- Add fish fillets, skin side down.
- Spoon sauce over fillets, reduce heat to medium-low, cover and simmer 15 minutes or until fish is opaque throughout.
- Garnish with basil.

INDONESIA

Photo courtesy of Whole Planet Foundation's Daniel Zoltani.

Kai

Photos courtesy of Whole Planet Foundation's Daniel Zoltani.

Josephine, Fiji
BUSINESS: catering

Josephine is a microcredit client in the Fijian island of Viti Levu where Whole Foods Market sources yellowfin and bigeye tuna. Through Whole Planet Foundation's partner South Pacific Business Development Microfinance (Fiji) Ltd., Josephine runs a small catering business in Nausori Town. There have been little to no viable microfinance organizations that have successfully served the very poor in the South Pacific in a sustainable manner, especially women working outside the formal sector. Since its launch in 2000, South Pacific Business Development in Samoa was the first to successfully implement the Grameen model in the region which has a relatively small total population, low population density and accordingly a higher cost of operations. Due to its success, South Pacific Business Development has expanded opportunity throughout the Pacific including Tonga and Fiji. With a $400,000 grant from Whole Planet Foundation, South Pacific Business Development will offer collateral-free group lending in under or unserved areas of the Pacific, reaching nearly 2,000 women. Learn more about Josephine and other entrepreneurs at *wholeplanetfoundation.org*.

FRESH WATER MUSSELS WITH COCONUT

This is Josephine's recipe, prepared her way. Fresh water mussels are commonly eaten in Fiji, garnished with coconut milk and spicy chiles. Josephine is a microcredit client of Whole Planet Foundation's microfinance partner South Pacific Business Development Microfinance (Fiji) Ltd.

Mussels
Coconut meat, freshly shredded
Limes, juiced
Chiles, freshly minced
Salt, to taste

- Boil or steam the mussels.
- Combine the shredded coconut, one cup of water, a splash of lime juice and a pinch of salt.
- Blend together and filter to create a milky sauce.
- Garnish mussels with the coconut milk mixture and chiles.

FIJI

Ají de Carne

Marina, Bolivia

BUSINESS: market restaurant

Marina is a microcredit client in the remote Potosí region of Bolivia where Whole Foods Market sources quinoa through Alter Eco. Whole Planet Foundation's support of Pro Mujer will assist in reaching 3,000 new clients in three years. Marina is a widow at 57 years old and has four children ranging from 25 to 35 in age. She is a restaurateur in the central market of Bolivia, offering as many as 12 different dishes every day that she prepares herself except on weekends when her daughter might help. Marina wakes at three o'clock in the morning in the freezing cold to go to the marketplace and prepare breakfast. She will stay at the small restaurant through dinner, returning home only after sunset, to sleep and do it again, resting on Sundays. Marina rents space in her house during the day to diversify her business and not always rely on the inconsistent restaurant income. She has taken advantage of the health services offered by Pro Mujer and knows the importance of self care. Learn more about Marina and other entrepreneurs at *wholeplanetfoundation.org*.

Photos courtesy of Whole Planet Foundation's Evan Lambert.

WHOLE PLANET
FOUNDATION

SPICY BEEF RIBS

This is Marina's recipe of a traditional Bolivian dish known simply as **AJÍ DE CARNE,** or "spicy beef." Although the name of the dish is spicy, it is generally prepared very mild, so most people who enjoy spicy food consider it flavorful with a hint of spice. Marina is a microcredit client of Whole Planet Foundation's microfinance partner Pro Mujer in Bolivia.

1 pound beef ribs
1 red spicy onion
1 carrot
Spicy chile peppers
Garlic
Oil
Salt
Pepper
Cumin

- Boil beef for 30 minutes in a pressure cooker along with chopped spicy onion and carrot.
- When beef is cooked, add garlic.
- Grind chile peppers and cook with a bit of oil.
- Add peppers to beef and vegetable mixture.
- Season to taste using cumin, salt, pepper or more garlic.
- Continue to simmer the above all day long.
- Serve with potatoes and salad as pictured.
- Makes 4 servings.

BOLIVIA

Carne en Vaho

Maria, Nicaragua

BUSINESS: catering

Maria is a microcredit client in Nicaragua where Whole Foods Market sources Whole Trade® coffee through Allegro Coffee Company®. Maria has been a microentrepreneur with Whole Planet Foundation's partner Pro Mujer for 22 loan cycles, over five years. She is a leader in her group and community and is a mother of four. Her business is daily catering of traditional meals such as *Carne en Vaho*, which is beef cooked with cassava and plantains. On Sundays, Maria prepares about 40 servings of this popular traditional dish that consists of dried and salted beef, marinated with onions and lime and spices, cassava and both green and ripe plantains. The dish is traditionally prepared steamed in banana or other leaves over an open wood fire. Learn more about Maria and other entrepreneurs at *wholeplanetfoundation.org*.

Photos courtesy of Whole Planet Foundation's Evan Lambert.

WHOLE PLANET
FOUNDATION®

BRINED BEEF WITH CASSAVA AND PLANTAINS

This **CARNE EN VAHO** is Maria's recipe and a popular traditional dish that consists of dried and salted beef, marinated with onions and lime and spices, and cassava plantains, prepared her way. Maria uses dried orange as kindling to be environmentally friendly. Maria is a microcredit client of Whole Planet Foundation's microfinance partner Pro Mujer in Nicaragua.

Cassava or yuca

Beef (salted and dried, soaked in lime and onion overnight)

Naranjillas (orange limes)

Onions

Banana leaves

Plantains

Shredded cabbage

- Soak cassava in water overnight.

- Marinate beef in lime (naranjilla), onion and spices.

- Place banana leaves in the bottom of a large pot.

- Peel the cassava and place in the bottom of the pot on the top of the first layer of banana leaves.

- Peel plantains and place a layer on top of cassava.

- Place beef on top of cassava and plantains.

- Prepare the fire.

- Steam for 2 hours over a hot flame.

- Serve over banana leaves, then layer cassava, plantains, meat and add cabbage slaw on top.

NICARAGUA

RECIPES FOR THE ADVENTUROUS AND CURIOUS

SHARING CULINARY CULTURE

Pliek U

Eli, Indonesia

BUSINESS: family restaurant

Eli is a microcredit client in Sumatra, Indonesia where Whole Foods Market sources Whole Trade® coffee through Allegro Coffee Company®. Eli is an entrepreneur from Banda Aceh where she lives with her husband and their young daughter. Together they own a restaurant called *Pijay*, where they both spend the majority of each day cooking and serving customers. Through Whole Planet Foundation's partner KOMIDA, Eli is currently on her second loan in the amount of $218 over the duration of one year. In the past she has utilized microfinance loans to purchase ingredients and materials for the restaurant. However, certain circumstances have required her to use the majority of her current loan to repair the family motorcycle, which her husband uses in the evenings as a taxi service. She hopes to obtain a larger loan size next cycle to expand the menu at her restaurant. Learn more about Eli and other entrepreneurs at *wholeplanetfoundation.org*.

Photos courtesy of Whole Planet Foundation's Daniel Zoltani.

SPICY INDONESIAN CURRY

Eli prepares this traditional curry her way, using **PLIEK U**, a traditional spice of Aceh, Indonesia. Eli is a microcredit client of Whole Planet Foundation's microfinance partner KOMIDA in Indonesia.

Pliek U
Salt
Cayenne peppers
Garlic
Shallots
Coriander
Cumin
Ground ginger
Ground turmeric
Peanuts
Shrimp
Papaya
Coconut milk
Lemongrass
Lime leaves
Spring onions
Galangal
Green, red and dried chiles
Rice, for serving

- Soak Pliek U in hot water about 10 minutes.
- Drain, rinse with cold water and grind until smooth.
- Heat water in a large wok.
- Add Pliek U, salt and spices.
- Add peanuts and shrimp.
- Slowly pour in coconut milk.
- Add remaining ingredients and cook until done.
- Serve with rice.

Photo courtesy of Whole Planet Foundation's Evan Lambert.

INDONESIA

Ika Loloi

Toutai, Tonga

BUSINESS: making and selling woven mats

Toutai is a microcredit client in the Ha'apai Islands of Tonga where Whole Foods Market sources yellowfin and bigeye tuna. Toutai is an entrepreneur from the Kuolo community in Ha'apai, where she lives with her husband and their three children. She runs a small business making and selling woven mats made from the leaves of the Pandanus palm. Traditionally, the leaves are prepared by stripping the thorny edges and laying them in the sun, or soaking them in saltwater, to bleach the color. Once dry and lighter in color they are then split into strips for weaving. These mats are symbolic of treasured heirlooms, articles of prestige and "some of the most traditional and important objects in Tonga," as described by Toutai. Through Whole Planet Foundation's partner South Pacific Business Development Microfinance (Tonga) Ltd., Toutai is currently on her first loan, which she used to purchase materials and hire extra weavers to meet the demand of her sales. She sells her mats to friends and relatives in New Zealand who use them for special events such as birthdays and weddings. Last year she sold five mats for 6,000 TOP ($3,426 USD). Learn more about Toutai and other entrepreneurs at *wholeplanetfoundation.org*.

Photos courtesy of Whole Planet Foundation's Daniel Zoltani.

BAKED FISH WITH BANANAS AND COCONUT MILK

This is Toutai's recipe and a favorite main dish traditionally made and served in Tonga, prepared her way. The cooked banana resembles and is described by many locals as cheese, which "melts" over a fresh fish fillet, marinated in lemon and cooked in coconut milk. Toutai is a microcredit client of Whole Planet Foundation's microfinance partner South Pacific Business Development Microfinance (Tonga) Ltd.

1 fish fillet
5 lemons, juiced
2 ripe bananas, thickly chopped
8 sprigs of green onions, chopped
1 cup of coconut milk

- Marinate fish in lemon juice for 5 minutes, or until the fish turns a whitish color.
- Place slices of one banana on a sheet of foil or banana leaf.
- Sprinkle a thin layer of green onions, and then place the marinated fish on top.
- Spread the remainder of the green onions on the top side of the fish and cover with remaining plantain slices.
- Add coconut milk and wrap tightly with foil or banana leaves.
- Bake in a hot oven for 30 minutes or until cooked through.

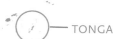
TONGA

Makloubeh

Photos courtesy of Whole Planet Foundation's Brian Doe.

Tisaam, Israel

BUSINESS: home-based catering

Tisaam is a microcredit client in northern Israel where Whole Foods Market sources paprika through Frontier-Co-op®. Through Whole Planet Foundation's partner KIEDF, Tisaam obtained a group guaranteed loan through KIEDF's Sawa program. KIEDF has been assisting small businesses to secure bank loans since 1994 and became the first microfinance non-bank direct lending organization in Israel in 2006. Inspired by the Grameen model, they offer group solidarity lending in rural Bedouin and Arab communities and within Jewish populations with a focus on poor women. Learn more about Tisaam and other entrepreneurs at *wholeplanetfoundation.org*.

WHOLE PLANET
FOUNDATION®

UPSIDE DOWN RICE WITH FRIED CHICKEN

This **Makloubeh** is Tisaam's recipe which means "flip it over," prepared her way like paella. Tisaam is a microcredit client of Whole Planet Foundation's microfinance partner KIEDF in Israel.

Chicken
Rice
Cauliflower
Carrots
Potatoes
Nutmeg
Cinnamon
White pepper
Salt

- Fry the chicken pieces.
- In a large pot, stack the chicken pieces, raw rice and vegetables.
- Season with nutmeg, cinnamon, white pepper and salt.
- Cover with water and simmer for about an hour, until the water boils off.
- Then *maloobi*, or flip it over, and cover with toasted almonds.
- When ready to serve, place a platter over the pot and flip it over so the components mix together.
- Serve warm.

ISRAEL

Tamales

Josefina, Mexico

BUSINESS: arts and crafts store

Josefina is a microcredit client of Whole Planet Foundation's partner Pro Mujer in Mexico where Whole Foods Market sources Whole Trade® peppers and tomatoes. Josefina (at left in the photo, pictured with her sister Patti) runs an arts and crafts store in Guanajuato and has a reputation of making traditional, delicious tamales. Josefina is on her second loan, which she uses for ingredients to make her tamales from scratch. She prepares two different kinds of tamales, one with a red sauce and pork, and the other with a green sauce and chicken, and she sells about 700-800 tamales per week in her neighborhood. She also exports to Austin, Texas when ordered by her customers there. Learn more about Josefina and other entrepreneurs at *wholeplanetfoundation.org*.

Photos courtesy of Whole Planet Foundation's Evan Lambert.

CHICKEN OR PORK TAMALES

This is Josefina's **TAMALE** recipe. It's a traditional and popular Mexican food dish that consists of cornmeal, lard, soup (using pork bones and/or a chicken carcass), and cheese (optional in the chicken recipe), steamed and wrapped in corn husks and prepared her way from scratch—a process that can take up to 14 hours. Josefina is a microcredit client of Whole Planet Foundation's microfinance partner Pro Mujer in Mexico.

Cornmeal, freshly ground that day
Yeast
Lard
Salt
Pork or chicken
Cheese (optional for chicken recipe)
Ground cascabel chile powder (red for pork)
Tomatillos (green for chicken)
Corn husks

- Cook chicken or pork.

- Keep the broth.

- Prepare the dough.

- Start with freshly ground cornmeal, add lard, salt, broth and yeast and mix by hand.

- Drop a small ball of dough into a glass of water. If it floats, it's ready.

- Prepare the chiles (for pork) or tomatillos (for chicken).

- Prepare the corn husks by soaking in water to soften.

- Fill with dough, then add the meat and chili sauce.

- Steam on a high flame for 2 hours in the winter, or 1½ hours during summer.

MEXICO

Mixiote

Maria, Mexico

BUSINESS: selling sweets and catering

Maria is a microcredit client in Mexico where Whole Foods Market sources Whole Trade® peppers and tomatoes. Pro Mujer provides poor women in Latin America with the means to build livelihoods for themselves and futures for their families through microfinance, business training and health care support. Maria sells sweets in front of the local school, as well as used clothing imported from her children living in the United States. She also makes food for special occasions such as the popular *Mixiote*, a traditional Mexican dish. Whole Planet Foundation is alleviating poverty through a partnership with Pro Mujer in Mexico, Nicaragua, Argentina, Bolivia and Peru, with more than $2 million of financial support committed. Pro Mujer is motivated to help a poor family move—in one generation—from having nothing to being able to provide their children with a financially secure, bright future. Learn more about Maria and other entrepreneurs at *wholeplanetfoundation.org*.

Photos courtesy of Whole Planet Foundation's Steve Wanta.

WHOLE PLANET
FOUNDATION®

CHICKEN IN CORN HUSKS

This **MIXIOTE** recipe is Maria's recipe and a traditional dish consisting of chicken slow cooked and wrapped in corn husks, with potatoes and **CHILE NOPAL**, or cactus chilies. Traditionally the wrapping, also known as a **MIXIOTE**, is the outermost layer of a maguey leaf, but Maria uses corn husks too. Maria is a microcredit client of Whole Planet Foundation's microfinance partner Pro Mujer in Mexico.

Ancho chiles
Guajillo chiles
Cactus chiles
Onions
Garlic cloves
Cinnamon sticks
Oregano
Thyme
Salt
Pepper
Chicken
Potatoes
Corn husks
Rice, for serving

- Heat water in the steamer pot on medium, uncovered, so that it warms up while you prepare the mixiotes.

- Soak chiles in boiling water until they have softened, approximately 10 minutes.

- Place the chiles in a blender and add onion, garlic, cinnamon, oregano, thyme, salt and pepper.

- Liquefy the ingredients with a little of the water in which the chiles were soaked. Grind until the salsa is smooth and thick.

- Pour the salsa into a glass container, add chicken and potatoes and mix well, making sure that all meat is covered with the sauce. Marinate for at least one hour in the refrigerator.

- Meanwhile, soak the corn husks or mixiote leaves. Once they are softened, fill with chicken, potatoes and salsa. Tie with a string.

- Place the mixiotes in a steamer with boiling water and cook, covered, until the chicken and potatoes are cooked, approximately 45 minutes.

- Remove the string and serve with rice.

MEXICO

Ếch xào là lốt

Photos courtesy of Whole Planet Foundation's Daniel Zoltani.

Nguyen, Vietnam

BUSINESS: restaurant

Nguyen is a microcredit client of Whole Planet Foundation's partner Tao Yeu Mai in the Phu Binh district in northeastern Vietnam where Whole Foods Market sources cinnamon through Frontier Co-op®. Nguyen owns and operates a restaurant with her husband. She was formally issued a loan from a commercial bank but found the interest rates were too high to successfully repay the amount based on the profits from her restaurant. She has since discovered the option of microcredit from Tao Yeu Mai and has received two consecutive one-year loans for her business. Nguyen has always been a strong leader in her community, and after obtaining her first loan, empowered other women in her district to apply and receive microcredit loans. Like many other restaurateurs, Nguyen uses the funds from her loans to purchase food and supplies for her now successful restaurant. Learn more about Nguyen and other entrepreneurs at *wholeplanetfoundation.org*.

WHOLE PLANET FOUNDATION®

FRIED FROG WITH GRAPE LEAVES

This **ẾCH XÀO LÀ LỐT** is Nguyen's recipe and is a storied Vietnamese meal about a poor couple living together in a hut near a rice paddy field. Visit *wholeplanetfoundation.org* for the story. Nguyen is a microcredit client of Whole Planet Foundation's microfinance partner Tao Yeu Mai in Vietnam.

2 pounds frog meat (chicken is an alternative)
Salt
Vegetable oil
1 clove garlic, chopped
Touch of chile, chopped
1 piece lemongrass root, chopped
1 ounce là lốt (grape leaves)
¼ cup soy sauce
Crushed pepper

Dipping sauce:
Ginger
Chile
½ teaspoon sugar

- To prepare frog meat, remove the heads of the frogs.
- Rub salt into the body to make it clean.
- Slightly cut the back of frog and peel off the skin.
- Remove the entrails and discard.
- Cut the frog meat into small pieces.
- Clean the meat with water and wait until it drains.
- Fry the meat in oil until it looks crispy, then strain to drain off oil.
- Add garlic, chile and lemongrass root and fry until crispy.
- Add the frog meat and briefly sauté.
- Slice grape leaves and add to the pan with soy sauce and salt.
- Prepare the sauce to serve as a dip. Slice ginger and chile together with sugar. Add a small amount of boiling water into the sauce and stir.
- Serve hot.

VIETNAM

RECIPES FOR THE ADVENTUROUS AND CURIOUS · SHARING CULINARY CULTURE

Travel with us from Honduras and Paraguay to Chile, over to Malawi, to Bangladesh, Thailand, Sri Lanka, the Philippines and Samoa with Brian Doe, Evan Lambert and Daniel Zoltani to enjoy sweets from the Americas, Africa and Asia. Whole Planet Foundation's programs team personally visits each microfinance organization to evaluate and monitor the partner's performance in serving the very poor. On his visit to Whole Planet Foundation's microfinance partner Small Enterprise Development in Thailand, Daniel met microcredit clients like Taunjai and her family and friends (pictured left). In addition to site visits, the team analyzes quarterly data from each microfinance partner supported by Whole Planet Foundation. Getting to know clients like Taunjai and understanding her loan utilization, repayment capacity and plans for the future is an important part of the work of the field team. It is this direct support of impoverished people that enables Whole Foods Market to give back to communities that supply the company with products such as rice from Surin, Thailand. Enjoy these goodies!

Top photo courtesy of Small Enterprise Development.
Bottom left photo courtesy of Whole Planet Foundation's Daniel Zoltani.
Bottom right photo courtesy of Whole Planet Foundation's Brian Doe.
Opposite Page: Photo courtesy of Whole Planet Foundation's Daniel Zoltani.

BAKED GOODS & DESSERTS

Pan de Coco

Photos courtesy of Whole Foods Market's Ha Lam.

Euceria, Honduras

BUSINESS: bread making

Euceria is a microcredit client in Honduras where Whole Foods Market sources coffee through Allegro Coffee Company®. Through Adelante Foundation, Whole Planet Foundation's partner in Honduras, small loans are offered to poor working women so that they can invest in their own businesses. Euceria makes *pan de coco* (coconut bread) and *pan dulce* (sweet bread), both staples of the regional diet. She has invested her first loan in ingredients for cooking, including flour, lard and salt. Euceria prepares the dough in her kitchen and cooks the bread over a fire pit outside of her home, using recipes and techniques she learned from her mother who was also a bread maker. She puts the warm rolls in a basket and walks through the streets of her community, selling her bread to neighbors. Learn more about Euceria and other entrepreneurs at *wholeplanetfoundation.org*.

WHOLE PLANET
FOUNDATION®

COCONUT BREAD

Whole Foods Market® tested recipe

SERVES 8

This Honduran staple, known as **PAN DE COCO,** is like a plump dinner roll. It's delicious served alongside a meal of rice, beans and fried plantains. Or enjoy it with your morning cup of coffee. This recipe was inspired by Euceria, a microcredit client of Whole Planet Foundation's first microfinance partner in Honduras, Adelante Foundation.

½ cup unsweetened finely grated coconut

2 tablespoons sugar

1 (0.25-ounce) package active dry yeast

½ cup warm water

3½ cups all-purpose flour, more for kneading

¾ teaspoon salt

1 cup coconut milk

3 tablespoons butter or non-hydrogenated vegetable shortening, melted

- Put coconut, sugar, yeast and water into a small non-reactive bowl and stir briefly. Set aside until mixture is swollen and bubbly, about 15 minutes.

- Mix flour and salt together in a large bowl. Add yeast mixture, coconut milk and butter. Using your hands or a wooden spoon, stir until well combined.

- Turn dough out onto a well-floured surface and knead, dusting with more flour as necessary, until soft and elastic, 5 to 6 minutes.

- Form dough into a ball, dust generously all over with flour and transfer to a clean large bowl.

- Cover bowl with a kitchen towel and set aside in a warm spot to let rise until doubled in size, about 1½ hours.

- Divide dough into 8 pieces and roll each into a ball.

- Arrange balls of dough on a large oiled baking sheet, spacing them 3 to 4 inches apart.

- Set aside in a warm spot, uncovered, to let rise until doubled in size again, about 45 minutes.

- Preheat the oven to 350°F. Bake bread until deep golden brown and cooked through, 20 to 25 minutes. Serve warm or set aside to let cool to room temperature.

HONDURAS

Caballitos, Casabe or Pan de Yuca

Photos courtesy of Whole Planet Foundation's Evan Lambert.

Doris, Honduras

BUSINESS: baking and selling bread and treats

Doris is a microcredit client in the Colon region of Honduras where Whole Foods Market sources coffee through Allegro Coffee Company®. Doris is a proud leader and part of the very first group formed in the Garifuna community called Punta Piedra. Her businesses is the making and selling of traditional Garifuna treats like *Pan De Coco*, cassava bread and the delicious gingerbread *Caballitos* which means "little horses." In her own words, she says that she makes "the best caballitos in town" which she believes is part of the reason for her growing success. While she primarily bakes and sells breads, she also sells gas and sodas for additional income. Though she has never had access to credit previously, nor does she have any collateral, she took her first loan of $50 through Whole Planet Foundation's partner FAMA and is now on her third loan of $200. She is a strong voice in the community, encouraging other women to form or join their own borrower groups. She has six children and dreams of a better life for them. She is determined and proud to be taking steps to better their financial situation to make these dreams a reality. Learn more about Doris and other entrepreneurs at *wholeplanetfoundation.org*.

HONDURAN GINGER CAKE

Whole Foods Market® tested recipe

(SERVES 16)

This simple treat is inspired by a popular cake made in Honduras. Fresh ginger gives it a subtle heat and grated cassava is the secret ingredient that adds a chewy texture. This recipe was inspired by Doris, a microcredit client of Whole Planet Foundation's microfinance partner FAMA in Honduras.

2 cups all-purpose flour
2 teaspoons baking powder
1 cup sugar
1 cup canola oil
1 cup grated cassava or yuca
4 teaspoons grated fresh ginger

- Preheat the oven to 350°F. Line an 8x8-inch baking pan with a long sheet of parchment paper, allowing for 2-inch overhang on each side.

- In a large bowl, whisk together flour and baking powder.

- In a separate bowl, whisk together sugar, oil, cassava and ginger.

- Whisk sugar mixture into flour mixture until blended.

- Spread batter into the prepared pan.

- Bake about 45 minutes or until golden and a toothpick inserted in center of cake comes out clean. Let cool completely.

- Remove cake from the pan and cut into squares.

HONDURAS

Nsima

Felicia, Malawi

BUSINESS: making and selling corn patties

Felicia is a microcredit client from outside Blantyre in southern Malawi where Whole Foods Market sources Whole Trade® sugar. Malawi ranks among the world's least developed countries and one of the most densely populated countries where over 85 percent of the population depends on subsistence agriculture. Through Whole Planet Foundation's partner MicroLoan Foundation, Felicia's loan in 2012 was $45. In 2013, her loan was $50, so she didn't increase her loan in real terms, but given the hard times facing the Malawian economy and sharp inflation last year, she is moving along with her corn muffin business. She is in her fifth loan cycle now and has a permanent selling location in the weekly market, whereas before she would migrate with her muffins wherever she could sell them. That has brought stability to her business and is the first step to being able to expand the business to other products in the future. Learn more about Felicia and other entrepreneurs at *wholeplanetfoundation.org*.

Photos courtesy of Whole Planet Foundation's Steve Wanta.

MALAWIAN CORN PATTIES

Whole Foods Market® tested recipe

SERVES 4

These dense corn cakes take their origins from a native dish from Malawi. Serve with a hearty soup or stew. This recipe was inspired by Felicia, a microcredit client of Whole Planet Foundation's microfinance partner MicroLoan Foundation in Malawi.

1 cup finely ground yellow cornmeal, divided
¾ teaspoon coarse sea salt

- Place ½ cup of the cornmeal in a medium saucepot and cook over medium-high heat about 5 minutes or until lightly toasted, stirring occasionally.

- Slowly add 2 cups water and salt and bring to a boil, stirring occasionally.

- Reduce heat to medium and gradually add remaining ½ cup cornmeal while stirring constantly and vigorously until mixture is very thick and dense, about 10 minutes.

- Remove from heat and use a clean spoon to scoop out 4 patties.

MALAWI

Photo courtesy of Whole Planet Foundation's Brian Doe.

Vaisalo

Agnes, Samoa

BUSINESS: raising livestock and mowing lawns

Agnes is a microcredit client in Samoa where Whole Foods Market sources yellowfin and bigeye tuna. Through Whole Planet Foundation's partner South Pacific Business Development (Samoa), Agnes used her first loan to buy herself a boar as she already had a sow and wanted to have baby pigs to raise and sell. She also bought wire to make a duck cage to help her raise ducks. She has had two more loans since then which she used to purchase a lawn mower that she now rents out to her neighbors for a profit. Agnes likes sharing *Vaisalo* as a morning breakfast dish because it is thought to give extra energy to the weak and strong health to the sick. Learn more about Agnes and other entrepreneurs at *wholeplanetfoundation.org*

Top photo courtesy of Whole Foods Market's Ha Lam.
Bottom photo courtesy of Whole Planet Foundation's Daniel Zoltani.

SAMOAN COCONUT TAPIOCA PORRIDGE

Whole Foods Market® tested recipe

SERVES 4

Inspired by the Samoan dish **VAISALO**, which is made with fresh coconut meat and starch, this warm tapioca porridge can be enjoyed for breakfast or dessert. The hint of sweetness and coconut is complemented by the chewy texture of tapioca. This recipe was inspired by Agnes, a microcredit client of Whole Planet Foundation's microfinance partner South Pacific Business Development Microfinance (Samoa) Ltd.

¼ cup small-pearl tapioca
1 (13.5-ounce) can light coconut milk
⅓ cup sugar
1½ teaspoons lemon juice
½ cup toasted unsweetened coconut flakes

- Place tapioca and 2 cups water into a medium heavy-bottomed saucepan and let soak 30 minutes.

- Add coconut milk and sugar; bring to a boil over medium heat, stirring constantly.

- Reduce heat to a simmer and cook about 15 minutes, or until tapioca is translucent, stirring frequently to prevent scorching.

- Stir in lemon juice and garnish with coconut flakes.

SAMOA

Photo courtesy of Whole Planet Foundation's Daniel Zoltani.

Kusli

Photos courtesy of Whole Planet Foundation's Daniel Zoltani.

Muslima, Bangladesh
BUSINESS: raising dairy cattle

Muslima is a microcredit client from the Rajshahi Division of northwest Bangladesh. Bangladesh is eligible for Whole Planet Foundation partnership because Whole Foods Market sells Teatulia Organic Teas whose single-source tea originates in northern Bangladesh. Through Whole Planet Foundation's partner Grameen Motsho O Pashusampad Foundation, Muslima is able to raise cattle and sell milk as her primary business. The overall objective of this microlending project is to reduce poverty by providing a model for sustainable rural development through livestock-based income generating activities and offering loans for purchasing a cow, goats, poultry and cattle. Additionally, education and technical training concerning the livestock is made readily available. Furthermore, support services enable clients to diversify their income within the livestock sector as an integrated system of activities. Learn more about Muslima and other entrepreneurs at *wholeplanetfoundation.org*.

CURRANT AND COCONUT CAKES

Whole Foods Market® tested recipe

SERVES 6

These sweet pastries from Bangladesh are stuffed with a buttery and satisfying blend of ingredients. Browning semolina flour in ghee develops a wonderfully nutty flavor that complements the almond flour and currants. This recipe was inspired by Muslima, a microcredit client of Whole Planet Foundation's microfinance partner Grameen Motsho O Pashusampad Foundation in Bangladesh.

6 tablespoons melted clarified butter (ghee), divided
¼ cup semolina
⅓ cup confectioners' sugar
⅓ cup currants
¼ cup almond flour
2 tablespoons grated unsweetened coconut
½ teaspoon ground cardamom
1 cup all-purpose flour
Pinch fine sea salt
4 to 5 tablespoons water
½ cup canola oil

- In a large skillet, heat 4 tablespoons of the butter over medium-high heat. Add semolina and cook 3 to 4 minutes or until just beginning to brown. Transfer to a large mixing bowl and let cool.

- Add sugar, currants, almond flour, coconut and cardamom and stir until evenly blended.

- Place flour and salt in a large bowl and stir in remaining 2 tablespoons butter. Stir in just enough water (about 4 to 5 tablespoons) to make stiff dough. Knead gently until smooth and cut into 6 equal pieces.

- Roll each piece of dough into small round circles 5-inches in diameter. (It is best to use the dough immediately after you have made it; letting it stand will make it soft. If the dough has become soft, knead in a little more flour until the dough is firm again.)

- Place about 2 tablespoons of the semolina mixture in the center of each dough circle (press semolina mixture together to firm up). Brush outside edge of dough with water and fold in half over filling. Press firmly to seal.

- In a large skillet, heat oil over medium-high until hot (you should have ¼-inch layer of oil). Add cakes and cook 3 to 4 minutes per side or until dough is cooked through and golden brown and crisp. Adjust heat as needed if oil becomes too hot. Cool and serve.

BANGLADESH

Blueberry Kuchen

Maria Angelica, Chile

BUSINESS: pastry shop

Maria Angelica is a microcredit client in the Temuco region of Chile where Whole Foods Market sources blueberries. Through Whole Planet Foundation's partner Fundación Banigualdad, Maria was able to purchase a large mixer for her pastry business, whose main focus is customer service. Maria has three daughters, and she and her family work as a team to make her business successful. Maria says it takes compromise, dedication and excellence, with the goal of creating happy customers who will return, which is her golden rule. Learn more about Maria and other entrepreneurs at *wholeplanetfoundation.org*.

Photos courtesy of Whole Planet Foundation's Evan Lambert.

WHOLE PLANET
FOUNDATION

CHILEAN BLUEBERRY TART

Whole Foods Market® tested recipe

SERVES 8–10

KUCHEN, a traditional German dessert, is found all over Chile in varying forms thanks to a large German community. This simple version features fresh blueberries mixed with blueberry jam for an easy topping. This recipe was inspired by Maria, a microcredit client of Whole Planet Foundation's partner Fundación Banigualdad in Chile.

6 tablespoons unsalted butter, melted; plus more for the pan

2 cups sifted all-purpose flour

1 teaspoon baking powder

2 eggs

⅔ cup sugar

⅔ cup milk

1 (6-ounce) package fresh blueberries

½ cup blueberry jam or preserves

¼ cup heavy cream, chilled

1 tablespoon confectioners' sugar

- Preheat the oven to 350°F. Lightly butter a 10- or 11-inch tart pan with a removable bottom.

- In a small bowl, whisk together flour and baking powder.

- In a separate large bowl, whisk together melted butter, eggs and sugar.

- Add flour mixture to butter mixture, alternating with milk and whisking until blended.

- Spread batter in the prepared tart pan.

- Bake 28 to 30 minutes or until a toothpick inserted in center comes out clean.

- Let cool completely on a wire rack.

- Meanwhile, in a small bowl, stir together blueberries and blueberry jam.

- Place cream and sugar in a bowl, and beat with an electric mixer just until stiff peaks form.

- Spread blueberry mixture on cake and decorate with whipped cream.

CHILE

Photo courtesy of Whole Planet Foundation's Evan Lambert.

Bibingka

Helen, Philippines

BUSINESS: raising pigs and rice cultivation

Helen is a microcredit client of Whole Planet Foundation's partner Negros Women for Tomorrow Foundation in Ormoc, Eastern Visayas in the Philippines where Whole Foods Market sources coconut oil, dried coconut and banana chips. The Negros Women for Tomorrow Foundation is named after Negros Island in the Philippines, named by the Spaniards because of the dark skin of the people who populated the island. Helen is from Ipil, one of the *barangays* in Ormoc City, the native Filipino term for village or district. She makes *Bibingka*, a traditional, sweet cake made from rice flour and sells them for 25 cents each. With her three sequential loans including her most current loan of $220, Helen purchased four piglets and operates a small rice field. An adjoining plot of land also serves as an additional income generating source. Helen says that her various businesses rotate depending on the season and her cash flow. Learn more about Helen and other entrepreneurs at *wholeplanetfoundation.org*.

Photos courtesy of Whole Planet Foundation's Daniel Zoltani.

WHOLE PLANET
FOUNDATION®

FILIPINO COCONUT RICE CAKE

Whole Foods Market® tested recipe

(SERVES 12)

This rich, sweet cake is based on the classic cake known as **BIBINGKA** in the Philippines. The cake is traditionally baked in a clay pot lined with banana leaves and heated in a charcoal oven. Banana leaves are a nice touch but not necessary—an oiled pan or individual oiled cups also work. This recipe was inspired by Helen, a microcredit client of Whole Planet Foundation's microfinance partner Negros Women For Tomorrow Foundation in the Philippines.

Banana leaves or canola spray oil, for the baking dish
1 (14-ounce) can coconut milk
1 cup light brown sugar
2 teaspoons (¼-ounce package) active dry yeast
2 cups rice flour
3 large eggs
½ teaspoon pure vanilla extract
⅛ teaspoon fine sea salt
½ cup fresh grated coconut meat or thinly sliced dried young coconut

- Preheat the oven to 350°F.

- Line a 9x13-inch baking dish or 12 (1-cup) ramekins or large muffin cups with banana leaves or spray with canola spray oil.

- Heat coconut milk briefly until it is just warm to the touch (105°F to 110°F).

- Transfer to a large bowl and whisk in brown sugar and yeast.

- Let set until mixture is bubbly, about 5 minutes.

- Beat in rice flour, eggs, vanilla and salt, beating until very smooth, about 1 minute.

- Pour the mixture into the prepared pan or ramekins and sprinkle with coconut.

- Bake until the edges are brown and the middle of cake is just set, 15 to 20 minutes for ramekins or about 25 minutes for a baking dish.

- Let cool a few minutes, cut into squares or unmold and serve warm or at room temperature.

PHILIPPINES

Photo courtesy of Whole Planet Foundation's Daniel Zoltani.

Payesh

Alokdia, Bangladesh

BUSINESS: dairy

Alokdia is a microcredit client of Whole Planet Foundation's partner Grameen Motsho O Pashusampad Foundation in Bangladesh. Bangladesh is eligible for Whole Planet Foundation partnership because Whole Foods Market sells Teatulia Organic Teas whose single-source tea originates in northern Bangladesh. Alokdia is an entrepreneur from the Rajshahi Division of northwest Bangladesh where she lives with her husband and two children. Alokdia is 32 years old and apart from being an experienced cook, she is the proud owner of one cow, which provides income to aid in supporting her family through the production of milk. She sells her daily milk collection to a community co-op, which then sells it to local customers. Alokdia previously owned multiple cows which she also milked to generate income, however due to financial hardships she was compelled to sell her livestock. She is now starting fresh with one cow in the hopes of making enough profit to regain her livestock standing. Learn more about Alokdia and other entrepreneurs at *wholeplanetfoundation.org*.

Photos courtesy of Whole Planet Foundation's Daniel Zoltani.

WHOLE PLANET
FOUNDATION

RICE PUDDING

Whole Foods Market® tested recipe

SERVES 4-6

PAYESH, or rice pudding, is a traditional South Asian sweet dish typically served during a meal or enjoyed as a soothing dessert. This recipe was inspired by Alokdia, a microcredit client of Whole Planet Foundation's microfinance partner Grameen Motsho O Pashusampad Foundation in Bangladesh.

4 cups whole milk, divided
6 small cardamom pods, crushed
3 bay leaves
¼ cup basmati rice
¼ cup sliced almonds
¼ cup currants
⅓ cup sugar
2 teaspoons ground cinnamon
1 teaspoon fine sea salt
Sliced fresh mint or honey for garnish

- Combine 2 cups of the milk, 1 cup water, cardamom, bay leaves, rice, almonds and currants in a medium saucepan and bring to a boil.

- Lower heat and simmer, uncovered, until rice begins to absorb the liquid, about 30 minutes.

- Add remaining 2 cups milk and sugar and simmer until mixture thickens, about 30 minutes more.

- Stir in cinnamon and salt and remove from heat.

- Remove bay leaves and serve warm or cold.

- Garnish with mint or honey.

BANGLADESH

Mbejú

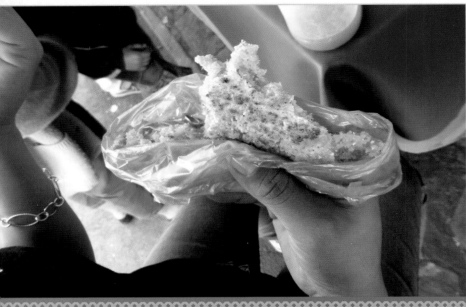

Photos courtesy of Whole Planet Foundation's Evan Lambert.

Celia and Olinda, Paraguay

BUSINESS: marketplace food stand

Celia is a microcredit client in the Villarrica region of Paraguay where Whole Foods Market sources sugar. Celia and her sister Olinda prepare typical Villarrican cuisine for sale in the downtown market. With a first loan of $125 and second loan of $250 through Whole Planet Foundation's partner Fundación Paraguaya, the sisters have increased the number and variety of dishes they sell, such as empanadas, fruit salad, sandwiches and cakes. Celia is showing us the typical dish *Mbejú*. Celia takes advantage of Fundación Paraguaya's *Club de Mujeres* (Women's Club) which offers benefits such as free monthly health screenings at participating clinics. Learn more about Celia, Olinda and other entrepreneurs at *wholeplanetfoundation.org*.

WHOLE PLANET
FOUNDATION

PARAGUAYAN CORN CAKE

This **MBEJÚ** is Celia's recipe of a Paraguayan staple food. Celia and her sister Olinda are microcredit clients of Whole Planet Foundation's microfinance partner Fundación Paraguaya in Paraguay.

Oil
Corn
Flour
Cheese
Milk
Honey

- Heat oil in a large skillet until very hot.
- Mix the remaining ingredients.
- Add a layer of the mixture into the pan, pushing the edges with the back of a utensil.
- Heat until evenly cooked.
- Using the lid of the pan, flip the Mbejú and finish cooking the same way as above.

PARAGUAY

Photo courtesy of Whole Planet Foundation's Evan Lambert.

Khanom Fuk Bau

Photos courtesy of Whole Planet Foundation's Daniel Zoltani.

Taunjai, Thailand

BUSINESS: silk weaving

Taunjai is a microcredit client in the Surin region of Thailand where Whole Foods Market sources rice through Alter Eco. Through Whole Planet Foundation's partner Small Enterprise Development Company, Taunjai is on her eighth loan, in the current amount of $330 and is paying interest of $6.60 plus a three percent service fee for each loan. Interest is paid monthly and a one-time payment of the loan principal is paid at the end of the loan term. Taunjai's monthly profit is approximately $660. From distribution of the textiles, Taunjai earns on average $1,000 per month and after expenses estimates an average monthly profit of $500-$660. For the next term, she plans to request a loan amount of $500 to begin increasing her business by purchasing woven materials from her village to sell to different markets in Bangkok. Her goal is to save enough money to buy a truck which would help facilitate the distribution of the textiles. Learn more about Taunjai and other entrepreneurs at *wholeplanetfoundation.org*.

FRIED LOTUS

This is Taunjai's **KHANOM FUK BAU** recipe and a traditional Thai dessert, prepared her way. A special ingredient is pandan juice, which is made by pressing the leaves of a green plant with fan-shaped sprays of long, narrow, blade-like leaves. Pandan juice has a unique taste and aroma and is used normally for desserts in Asian countries. Taunjai is a microcredit client of Whole Planet Foundation's microfinance partner Small Enterprise Development Company in Thailand.

2 cups raw regular rice flour
¼ cup raw sticky rice flour
½ cup sugar
Pinch salt
Pandan leaves
¼ teaspoon pandan juice
2 cups vegetable oil

- Whisk together 2 flours. In a separate bowl, mix 1/2 cup water with sugar and salt.
- Mash pandan leaves and mix with water.
- Filter and pour pandan juice into flour.
- Stir all ingredients together until thick and creamy.
- Set aside until the dough rises.
- Add oil to a wok or small deep pan. The pan should be small because the shape of the dessert will be more easily maintained.
- Once the oil is hot, use a spoon to scoop batter into the pan for frying.
- Once the edges of the pastry are a golden brown, flip over.
- Fry until the pastry is cooked throughout.
- Place on a grate to drain.
- Add a tablespoon of oil after making 4 to 5 pieces, with no need to change the oil. Repeat with remaining batter. Good luck!

THAILAND

Cassava Lidgid

Photos courtesy of Whole Planet Foundation's Daniel Zoltani.

Margie, Philippines

BUSINESS: catering, pig raising and vegetable farming

Margie is a microcredit client of Whole Planet Foundation's partner Negros Women for Tomorrow Foundation in Ormoc, Eastern Visayas in the Philippines where Whole Foods Market sources coconut oil, dried coconut and banana chips. Margie, an entrepreneur from the Leyte Island, operates several businesses beyond making and selling *Cassava Lidgid*, including a small plot of land where she raises pigs and grows pineapple, corn, bananas and eggplant for sale at the local market. Margie expresses the hardships of growing up with an alcoholic father who repeatedly used the family money for his habit, which compelled her to provide for the family at an early age. She regrets finishing only her third year of high school but felt it was necessary to generate additional income to support the family, as she is the oldest of her siblings. She often feels like she missed an opportunity to excel further because of her lack of education and therefore is making it a priority for her two sons. One of her sons is currently in high school and the other is studying to be a mechanical engineer. Learn more about Margie and other entrepreneurs at *wholeplanetfoundation.org*.

SHREDDED CASSAVA IN BANANA LEAVES

This **CASSAVA LIDGID** is Margie's recipe and a traditional sweet dessert made with shredded cassava and wrapped in banana leaves. Margie is a microcredit client of Whole Planet Foundation's microfinance partner Negros Women for Tomorrow Foundation in the Philippines.

1 sack shredded cassava or yuca
Banana leaves
Coconut milk
Sugar

- Squeeze cassava and remove the juice using a net or cloth.
- Pass banana leaves over a flame on both sides to make it easy to fold.
- In a bowl, mix cassava, coconut milk and sugar, until well blended.
- Scoop ¼ cup of the mixture and wrap tightly in a banana leaf, to make a thin roll shape.
- In a deep cooking pan, line with cut banana leaves and layered with the wrapped cassava mixture.
- Add water, enough to fill the pan above the wrapped cassava mixture.
- Cook in high fire or traditional oven for 1 hour.

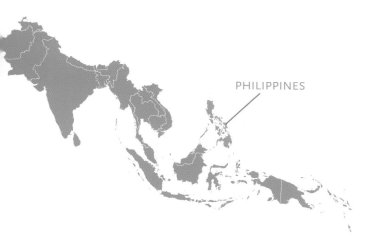

PHILIPPINES

Photo courtesy of Whole Planet Foundation's Daniel Zoltani.

Quench your thirst with **FRESH MANGO LIMEADE** from Nicaragua and head south to Peru for a **HOT QUINOA DRINK**, stop by Morocco for **MOROCCAN MINT TEA**, head to Israel for **CARDAMOM COFFEE** and Thailand for **THAI ICED TEA**, then finish in Nepal with a **NEPALESE TONGBA BEER** with Daniel Zoltani, Evan Lambert, Brian Doe, Joy Stoddard and Genie Bolduc. When Brian and Joy (pictured bottom left) visited Whole Planet Foundation's microfinance partner INMAA in Morocco, meetings with microcredit clients included mint tea served with flatbread, honey and jam. Fresh mint is essential to Moroccan mint tea, and the best part about its preparation is spending time together with your hosts while the head of the household infuses the tea. There are three successive infusions of the green tea, mint and sugar, each sweeter than the last. Traditionally, the tea is served in a polished teapot the host lifts up high and pours into the small glasses, which are carried on a metal tray. It is often garnished with pine nuts for special occasions. Whole Planet Foundation's Regional Director for Africa/ Middle East, Brian, lived on the continent of Africa for more than 10 years and is responsible for auditing, monitoring and supporting Whole Planet Foundation's microfinance partners in 20 countries, and drinking a lot of tea!

Top left photo courtesy of Whole Planet Foundation's Evan Lambert.
Bottom photo courtesy of Whole Planet Foundation's Genie Bolduc.
Opposite Page: Photo courtesy of Sophie Eckrich.

BEVERAGES

Chi Yen

Photos courtesy of Whole Planet Foundation's Daniel Zoltani.

Sunee, Thailand
BUSINESS: beverage cart

Sunee is a microcredit client in Thailand where Whole Foods Market sources rice through Alter Eco. Through her first loan with Whole Planet Foundation's partner Small Enterprise Development Company, Sunee owns and operates a beverage cart. With her first loan, she bought an attachment roof for her already owned motorcycle to begin selling beverages on the street. She says Thai iced tea is her best seller which she sells for 50 cents. She usually works from 7 o'clock in the morning to 5 o'clock in the evening each day generating a daily profit of $10. She likes the convenience and mobility of her work; if business is slow she has the freedom to move to another location. The loans now are used to buy the necessary stock of materials and ingredients in order to ensure demands from her customers are met. Learn more about Sunee and other entrepreneurs at *wholeplanetfoundation.org*.

THAI ICED TEA

Whole Foods Market® tested recipe

SERVES 4

A popular drink in both Thailand and Thai restaurants around the globe, this cold tea is sweetened with sugar then topped off with evaporated milk. Ceylon tea is a traditional choice but the drink can also be made with black tea or oolong. This recipe was inspired by Sunee, a microcredit client of Whole Planet Foundation's microfinance partner Small Enterprise Development Company in Thailand.

4 bags Ceylon tea *(Note: in Thailand, 4 tablespoons of loose Ceylon tea is preferred.)*
½ cup sugar
Ice cubes, for serving
1 cup evaporated milk

- In a large saucepan, bring 4 cups water to a boil.
- Add tea bags and remove from heat.
- Let steep 5 minutes.
- Strain tea into a large pitcher or bowl.
- Add sugar and stir to dissolve.
- Let cool to room temperature.
- Cover and refrigerate until chilled.

To serve:

- Fill 4 glasses with ice.
- Add enough tea to fill glasses leaving about 1 inch from top.
- Add ¼ cup evaporated milk to each glass and serve.

THAILAND

Agua Fresca de Mango

Top photo courtesy of Whole Foods Market's Ha Lam.
Bottom photo courtesy of Whole Planet Foundation's Evan Lambert.

Miriam, Nicaragua

BUSINESS: market stand

Miriam is a microcredit client in Nicaragua where Whole Foods Market sources Whole Trade® coffee through Allegro Coffee Company®. Through Whole Planet Foundation's partner Pro Mujer, Miriam is able to sell fruits and vegetables in the central market of Jinotega and also walks around with a bucket of beverages, selling on the bus and in traffic. Her loan size is $300, with eight payments over four months, and she is in a leadership position in her lending groups, known as Center Chief. Miriam belongs to the same borrower group as her daughter who is shown with her in the photo. The most impactful part of Pro Mujer for Miriam is that its health services detected an early diagnosis of cancer in her daughter, and they hope to have caught it in its early stages. Miriam also was sick, with a lung issue from burning wood inside on her cookstove, so she now cooks only with gas and for the past two years has been much more healthy. Miriam is a single mother with three kids and works from six o'clock in the morning until four o'clock in the afternoon, seven days a week. In the past, Miriam had credit with other lending institutions but she says the service is better with Pro Mujer. Miriam's dream is to build her own home someday with profits and savings. Learn more about Miriam and other entrepreneurs at *wholeplanetfoundation.org*.

FRESH MANGO LIMEADE

Whole Foods Market® tested recipe

SERVES 2

This light, refreshing drink popularized in Central America is a terrific thirst quencher on a hot summer day. **AGUA FRESCA** (Spanish for "fresh water") uses more water than a smoothie would in order to flavor the water and not just purée the fruit. This recipe was inspired by Miriam, a microcredit client of Whole Planet Foundation's microfinance partner Pro Mujer in Nicaragua.

1 ripe mango, cut into chunks
½ teaspoon freshly squeezed lime juice
½ teaspoon agave nectar or honey, more or less to taste
1 lime, cut into wedges
2 fresh mint sprigs for garnish

- In a blender, combine mango and 1½ cups cold water and blend until smooth.
- Pour through a strainer into ice-filled glasses.
- Stir in lime juice and agave.
- Garnish with lime wedges and mint, and serve.

NICARAGUA

Atai bi Nana

Mohammed, Morocco
BUSINESS: neighborhood café

Mohammed is a microcredit client in Morocco where Whole Foods Market sources spices and essential oils through Frontier Co-op®. Through Whole Planet Foundation's partner INMAA, Mohammed took a loan of $350 to open and operate a café near Tinghir in the Souss-Massa-Draâ region. Prior to the loan he was travelling around the region doing short term day labor, and of course spent a lot of time in cafés on breaks. He and a friend got the idea to start a café themselves in their hometown so they wouldn't have to travel from their families so much. He said he can bring in about $6 of profit a day with the business. Mohammed also rents out two rooms in the building to lodgers for extra income. Learn more about Mohammed and other entrepreneurs at *wholeplanetfoundation.org.*

Top left and bottom photos courtesy of Whole Planet Foundation's Steve Wanta.
Top right photo courtesy of Whole Planet Foundation's Genie Bolduc.

WHOLE PLANET
FOUNDATION®

MOROCCAN MINT TEA

Whole Foods Market® tested recipe

SERVES 6

Moroccans combine green tea, mint leaves and a hearty dose of sugar to make this traditional beverage. Mint tea is a beverage of hospitality in Morocco, served whenever guests arrive, as well as throughout the day. This recipe was inspired by Mohammed, a microcredit client of Whole Planet Foundation's microfinance partner INMAA in Morocco.

3 tablespoons loose green tea leaves or 5 green tea bags
1 bunch fresh spearmint leaves, plus extra for garnish
⅓ cup sugar or ¼ cup agave nectar, more to taste

- Bring 8 cups water to a boil in a large pot over high heat.
- Remove the pot from the heat and add tea.
- Cover and steep 4 to 5 minutes.
- Add mint to the pot.
- Cover and steep 5 minutes more.
- Add the sugar and stir to combine.
- Strain and serve.
- Garnish with a mint sprig.
- To serve chilled, allow the tea to reach room temperature, then transfer the tea to a pitcher, cover and refrigerate until cold.
- Serve in a tall glass with ice and a mint sprig for garnish.

MOROCCO

Bebida Caliente de Quinoa

Brigida, Peru

BUSINESS: beverage stand

Brigida is a microcredit client in Peru where Whole Foods Market sources quinoa and Whole Trade® bananas and mangoes. Through Whole Planet Foundation's partner Pro Mujer, Brigida operates a beverage stand in the morning market, selling a traditional Peruvian quinoa-based breakfast beverage. Whole Planet Foundation partners with Pro Mujer in Peru and also in Argentina, Bolivia, Mexico and Nicaragua, where they offer poor women in Latin America the means to build livelihoods for themselves and futures for their families through microfinance, business training and health care support. Learn more about Brigida and other entrepreneurs at *wholeplanetfoundation.org*.

Bottom photo courtesy of Sophie Eckrich.

WHOLE PLANET
FOUNDATION®

HOT QUINOA DRINK

Whole Foods Market® tested recipe

SERVES 4

A popular breakfast beverage in South America, make this mixture at night and reheat in the morning. It's a thick, slightly sweet drink full of nutrients and protein from the quinoa. This recipe was inspired by Brigida, a microcredit client of Whole Planet Foundation's microfinance partner Pro Mujer in Peru.

½ cup quinoa
2 cups soymilk
2 apples, peeled and quartered
2 tablespoons packed light brown sugar
½ teaspoon ground cinnamon
1 teaspoon pure vanilla extract

- Place quinoa and 2 cups water in a medium saucepan and bring to a boil.
- Reduce heat to low, cover and simmer 15 minutes or until quinoa is tender.
- Drain well.
- Return quinoa to the saucepan and add soymilk, apples, sugar and cinnamon.
- Bring to a simmer over medium-high heat.
- Reduce heat to medium and cook 5 minutes.
- Transfer mixture to a blender, add vanilla and purée until smooth.
- Serve hot.

PERU

Cafe Shahor with Heile

Tisaam, Israel

BUSINESS: home-based catering

Tisaam is a microcredit client in Karmi'el, Israel where Whole Foods Market sources paprika through Frontier Co-op®. Through Whole Planet Foundation's partner KIEDF, Tisaam obtained a group loan called the SAWA product with four other women. KIEDF has been assisting small businesses to secure bank loans since 1994 and became the first microfinance organization in Israel in 2007. Inspired by the Grameen model, they offer group solidarity lending in rural Bedouin and Arab villages with a focus on poor women. Learn more about Tisaam and other entrepreneurs at *wholeplanetfoundation.org.*

Bottom photo courtesy of Whole Planet Foundation's Brian Doe.

WHOLE PLANET
FOUNDATION®

CARDAMOM COFFEE

Whole Foods Market® tested recipe

(SERVES 12)

Strong coffee flavored with cardamom is popular in Israel and other parts of the Middle East. One method for making it is to simply drop whole cardamom pods into small cups of thick, rich coffee, and the other is to actually brew the coffee and cardamom together as in this versatile recipe. This recipe was inspired by Tisaam, a microcredit client of Whole Planet Foundation's microfinance partner KIEDF in Israel.

1½ teaspoons whole cardamom seeds (not pods)
1 cup (about 2½ ounces) dark-roast whole coffee beans
Sugar, to taste (optional)

- Grind cardamom seeds and coffee together and store in an airtight container.
- Brew the coffee using your regular method, or make traditional cooked coffee:
- Grind beans and cardamom very finely.
- Bring 1½ cups water to boil in a small pan (traditionally a long-handled cup-like pot called a *finjan* is used).
- Stir in ¼ cup coffee-cardamom mixture and sugar to taste.
- Cook over medium-low heat until liquid simmers around the edges and coffee grinds begin to sink, 2 to 3 minutes.
- Remove from heat and let set 1 minute.
- Pour coffee carefully into small cups, leaving most of the grounds behind in the pan.

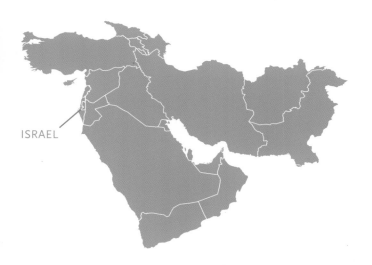

ISRAEL

Jaand

Esodada, Nepal

BUSINESS: small corner store

Esodada is a microcredit client in the eastern province of Mechi, Nepal where Whole Foods Market sources tea. Through Whole Planet Foundation's partner Nirdhan Utthan Bank, Esodada runs a corner store and loves to cook. Half of the Nepalese population has no access to even the most basic financial services. In rural areas, farming families are trapped in cycles of debt and are often forced to sell their crops at below market rates, slipping further into poverty. Learn more about Esodada and other entrepreneurs at *wholeplanetfoundation.org*.

Photos courtesy of Whole Planet Foundation's Daniel Zoltani.

NEPALESE TONGBA BEER

JAAND is a millet-based alcoholic beverage found in the far eastern mountainous region of Nepal. It is the traditional and indigenous drink of the Limbu and Rai people of eastern Nepal and has cultural and religious importance to them. TONGBA is the name of the vessel which holds the fermented alcoholic beverage known as JAAND, but the beverage is also commonly known as TONGBA these days. This recipe was inspired by Esodada, a microcredit client of Whole Planet Foundation's microfinance partner Nirdham Utthan Bank in Nepal.

Millet

Marcha, a fermenting agent, or use baker's fresh yeast (not dried)

NEPAL

- Wash and boil millet until it becomes soft.

- Cool millet and mix with *marcha*, a source of molds, bacteria and yeast.

- Collect the mash and place in a woven bamboo basket lined with green leaves or plastic, cover with a thick fold of cloth and store in a warm place for 1–2 days.

- Pack the sweet mash tightly into an earthenware pot or plastic jars, sealing the opening to prevent air from entering.

- After 7–15 days depending upon the temperature, the fermentation is complete and the mass is converted to *Jaand*. It should be kept warm but not too warm.

- To intensify the flavor of *Jaand*, leave it undisturbed and stored for about six months.

- To consume, put the fermented millet in a container, traditionally called a *Tongba*, and pour in boiled water to the brim.

- Leave undisturbed for about 5 minutes.

- Drink with a bamboo straw, perforated on the side to act as a filter. Insert the straw into the container to suck out the warm liquid from the millet grains.

- Add more hot water as the Tongba becomes dry, and repeat the process until the alcohol is exhausted.

ACKNOWLEDGEMENTS

*Whole Planet Foundation is grateful to these contributors of **LIBERATION SOUP**, our first cookbook. Thanks to their generosity and belief that microentrepreneurs around the globe can lift themselves out of poverty through their own hard work and creativity, this cookbook was made possible.*

WE WOULD LIKE TO EXPRESS OUR GRATITUDE TO:

Our microfinance partners around the world

Microentrepreneurs in 34 countries who inspired us with delicious dishes

Mambo Sprouts Marketing for their support in the process of creating the cookbook

Mambo Sprouts Marketing's Creative Director Taralynn Ross, for her design talent and unending enthusiasm

Whole Foods Market's Kate Rowe and Molly Siegler for their culinary editing and dedication; and Allison Kociuruba, Liz Pearson and Alice K. Thompson, for their recipe development

Whole Foods Market's Ha Lam and Marc Hamel for their photography support

Whole Foods Market's Liz Burkhart for promoting the cookbook

Whole Foods Market's Global Whole Body team of Maren Giuliano, Karen Alpers, Jeanne Tamayo, Susan Wattik and Nancy Dagnall for their support of retailing the book

Whole Foods Market's Guest Services and Whole Body teams for retailing the book

Whole Planet Foundation's Steve Wanta, Brian Doe, Evan Lambert and Daniel Zoltani, for their time spent in the field gathering recipes, photos and stories

Whole Planet Foundation's Genie Bolduc and Victor Quiroz for organizing assets

Whole Planet Foundation's Lauren Evans, Armando Huerta, Claire Kelly, Alyssa Manse, Daniel Vidal and JP Kloninger for proofreading

Please join us in appreciating all of our partners for investing in a future without poverty for more than four million people.

It is our sincere hope that everyone on the planet will flourish.

WHOLE PLANET
FOUNDATION